John Coleman

The rival queens

A story of the modern stage

John Coleman

The rival queens
A story of the modern stage

ISBN/EAN: 9783337291105

Printed in Europe, USA, Canada, Australia, Japan

Cover: Foto ©ninafisch / pixelio.de

More available books at **www.hansebooks.com**

▓▓▓▓▓▓▓▓▓▓▓ENS

A ST▓▓▓▓▓▓▓▓

IN THREE VOLUMES

BY

JOHN COLEMAN

Author of "Curly:—An Actor's Story" "Memoirs of Samuel Phelps"
"Reminiscences of Charles Reade" &c

"And one was far apart, and one was near:
 Ay, ay, O ay—the winds that bow the grass!
 And one was water, and one star was fire,
 And one will ever shine, and one will pass,
 Ay, ay, O ay—the winds that move the mere!"
                                           TENNYSON.

VOL I

London
REMINGTON AND CO PUBLISHERS
HENRIETTA STREET COVENT GARDEN

1887
[*All Rights Reserved*]

PROLOGUE.

THE WHITE LADYE OF ROSE-MOUNT.

BOOK THE FIRST.

CHAP.		PAGE
I.	Love, Lord of All...	25
II.	Romeo and Juliet...	42
III.	"The Girls they left Behind Them"	53

BOOK THE SECOND.

ROBERT PENARVON'S NARRATIVE.

CHAP.		PAGE
I.	Orestes and Pylades (A Retrospect)	73
II.	En Route to the East	88
III.	Herbert's Ordeal...	96
IV.	Miss Challoner	109
V.	My own Ordeal	137
VI.	Her Majesty's Servants	144
VII.	My First and Last Appearance as an Actor	156
VIII.	The Private Secretary	178
IX.	As You Like it	193
X.	The Legacy	203
XI.	The Passing of Fairfax	208
XII.	At Rest	221

PROLOGUE.

THE WHITE LADYE OF ROSEMOUNT.

> "Yet here for me, though heart and will are master
> As strong as iron and as calm as death,
> The will will waver, and the heart beat faster,
> Touched by the memory of a woman's breath."
> HERMAN MERIVALE.

PEOPLE said the Theatre House at Rosemount was haunted, and so it was—one room especially—a strange, weird room—a room with crannies and niches, and cupboards and cabinets, and a huge embayed window, in front of which stood the noblest minster in all broad England, perhaps in all the world.

Besides the choice pictures, the quaint furniture, and rare books, this room was filled with rarer memories.

If it could but speak, what strange stories it could tell!

In this house, more than a century ago, the poor nonjuring Savoy parson's famous son, whom beautiful, cruel Peg Woffington drove penniless from London, found a home.

Here, in this very room, he entertained the learned Bruin and obsequious Bozzy, on their way back from the Hebrides; and the Doctor smacked his lips over the larded capon and the good red wine, while he thanked God he was in a Christian land once more, and on his way back to Fleet Street.

Here jovial James Quin discussed John Dory, the Duke's venison, and the Bishop's claret with honest Tate.

Here the great little Davy (prince of actors and of gentlemen) "set the table on a roar" at the expense of insolent Sam Foote. Here young Dick Sheridan lost his last shilling at Faro, and then borrowed ten guineas to take him to town.

Here, too, the red-coated bullies demanded that gaunt John Kemble should apologize for becoming pretty Elizabeth Inchbald's champion, what time the brave lad, fresh from Douay, said, "My father is a gentleman, and my father's son can never be cajoled or coerced into an act unworthy of a gentleman. I will not apologize!"

Here great Sarah Siddons, descending from her pedestal, "took snuff sometimes, and sometimes tea."

Here, too, a wretched, ragged girl from Ireland, stood trembling before the despot of the North—a girl hereafter destined to witch all eyes and win all hearts, as the spirit of comedy incarnate, in the form of Dorothea Jordan.

Here reckless, dissolute George Frederick Cooke — and, later, the divine Edmund, greatest of actors and blackguards — became "o'er all the ills of life victorious."

Here John Emery, little Knight, Liston, and the elder Mathews came, quaking to hear the managerial verdict — actor or no actor?

Here Elliston, the Dean, and the manager, got "regal" together.

Here, too, in later days, gallant Charles Kemble, classic Charles Young, grim Macready, "Gladiator" Forrest, rare old Sam Phelps, genial Charles Kean, "Bucky" Ben Webster, the fascinating Fechter, the ever-young Charles Mathews, poor Gus Brooke, glorious Charles Dickens, and leonine Charles Reade have sat and laughed "o'er the walnuts and the wine," and many a time and oft have helped to speed the happy hours away.

Alas! the days that are no more!

Here, too, on this bleak winter's night, sat

Frank Fairfax, the manager of the Great Northern Circuit, reading the faces in the fire, and conjuring up, amidst the glowing embers, " the loved, the lost, the distant and the dead."

Suddenly a loud double " rat-tat " disturbed his reverie.

Footsteps on the stairs followed ; then a gentle tap at the door of the historic room here described.

" Come in," said the manager.

To him enters Brown, his valet, with a telegram.

" Any answer, sir ? "

" No."

" Please, sir, boy says, may he go into the pit ? "

" Oh, yes—that is, if there is any room." Then, looking at his watch, " Stop ! how came it that this was not delivered before ? "

" Boy said it was delayed in transmission,

in consequence of snow deranging wires, sir."

" Confound the snow! It may delay the train as well. We haven't a moment to lose. Go to the station, Brown. Mind you are there at a quarter to ten. Have a cab ready to meet the express from the North. There will be a young lady in the train—tall, slight, fair hair, dark eyes and eyebrows. You can't mistake her. Make my compliments—say I have had a busy day at Castletown or I would have met her myself. Bring her here.

"Stay! When you have brought her, run round to Mrs. Macnamara and secure Miss Vigo's rooms as soon as she leaves for Newcastle. Post these letters as you pass the post-office. Send these telegrams, and tell Mrs. Brown to come up immediately. Sharp's the word. Look alive." And off went Brown.

The manager sighed as he murmured —

"Twenty years ago! and yet it seems as if it were but yesterday!

"She was a flirt, and I was a fool; but *he,* at least, knew his own mind—the scoundrel!

"Yes, and he subdued her to his stronger will. If I had only spoken then!

"Ah! well—' He who will not, when he may —'"

Another tap at the door, and Mrs. Brown, the housekeeper, enters.

"Mrs. Brown," said Fairfax, "in an hour's time let me have a plate of soup, an omelette, a maccaroni cheese, a pint of mulled claret, and a bottle of Roederer. In an hour, you understand."

"Yes, sir."

"And tell Emma to clear my traps out, and put them in the Ghost Room."

"The G—ghost Room, sir?"

"Yes, and be sure there are roaring fires. A young lady, who is coming, will sleep in my room to-night, and I'll take the other."

"Lord, sir, you don't mean —"

"Yes, I do; so off you go, and be quick about the supper."

And away went Mrs. Brown, sorely exercised in her mind about her instructions.

The manager paced up and down in agitation, and half muttered to himself, half murmured aloud —

"Yes, it all comes back. We were to have met as usual on the top of the Calton Hill at two o'clock.

"I was at my post an hour before my time. The place was deserted. I sat looking at the blue Firth, counting the tardy minutes. Then I lighted a weed, and lost myself in a daydream—how happy we should be together—she and I.

"I was brought back to earth by voices—hers and *his*. The sound arose from beneath my feet, ever so far down below.

"I rose, and looked over the edge of the

precipice. I saw them—I can see them now—as he held her to his breast, and forced a ring upon her finger. I thought she seemed to struggle for one moment—but the next—their lips met—and then — !"

The very hour after that on which he discovered the treachery of his friend and the falseness of his sweetheart, Fairfax broke his engagement, shook the dust of Edinburgh from his feet, turned his face to the south, and from that time he never crossed the Border again—never again looked upon her face in life; and yet, even now, he saw a fair young girl and a boy strolling hand in hand together, plucking flowers on the Calton Hill on the young May morning, all those long years ago.

Then came the obverse of the picture. He, that other one—the false friend, the profligate, the drunkard—he who had embittered the life of her whom he had sworn to love and cherish.

"D—n him! Oh! d—n him!" exclaimed Fairfax, chafing with the memory of that unforgotten, unforgiven wrong.

After a time he paused and softened. Then he drew two letters from his breast coat pocket; the first was written in a feeble, feminine hand; it was blotted here and there, and ran thus:—

"DEAR FRANK,

"May I call you so once more for the sake of auld lang syne?

"Though so many years have passed since we parted, I have never lost sight of your bright career; I have always rejoiced in your triumphs, though, alas!— Well, well — you have been amply avenged by my most unhappy marriage.

"Long before I became a widow my sole consolation was my child, my little Clara, soon, I fear, to be left an orphan. She was eighteen last birthday. Though proud and impetuous, she is tender, truthful, and affectionate. I hope a mother's partiality does not mislead me, but I really think that there is a great future before her. My poor darling is eating her heart out in these obscure places, and she has made me write you.

"It has been a great effort, for I am very feeble to-day.

"Frank, dear Frank, you will help my poor child for 'Maria's' sake, won't you? I can write no more; it has become all at once so —"

Here the letter terminated abruptly.

The manager paused, overcome with emotion. After awhile, he read the other letter, which was written in bold and vigorous characters, and was to this effect:—

"Ivy Villa,
"Kilmarnock,
"December 18th, 187—.

"Dear Mr. Fairfax,

"I send you my mother's letter just

as she left it. After she had written the last line, she said to me —

"'It is very dark, my child.'

"Alas! The darkness was in her own eyes. An hour afterwards she had found the light!

"I am grateful to God that her sufferings are at an end; of late they have been more than she could endure, or I could bear to see.

"Your name was the last upon her lips.

"I feel how almost indelicate it may appear to broach such a subject at such a time, but I have now to face the world alone.

"If it should please you to entrust me with an engagement in your company, I will endeavour to merit your commendation.

"I am,
"Dear Mr. Fairfax,
"Most respectfully yours,
"CLARA TREVOR."

As he returned the letters to his breast, he murmured, "Poor child! Poor mother!"

More than twenty years ago Frank Fairfax made his first appearance at the Theatre Royal, Edinburgh, as Charles Surface.

On that occasion he met for the first time, Lucy Seymour. She was the "Maria" of the comedy; it is but a small part, but "amidst the follies, the vanities, the deceits and vices" of the fashionable crew of scandal-mongers by which she is surrounded, this simple country maiden stands out an angel of innocence and purity.

How well he recalled the young, frank, lovely face, the symmetrical figure, the simple white muslin frock, the bunches of black ribbon, the large Leghorn hat, the sunny glory of the golden hair, the lustrous, timid, dark eyes.

As he spoke the concluding lines—

> "Though thou, dear maid, shouldst waive thy beauty's sway,
> Thou still must rule, because I will obey,"

he stooped and kissed her hand. He could

see her now as she flushed to the temples, and looked up with her great wondering eyes into his—and then—he—

"Psha!" he exclaimed aloud, as he started up impatiently, "what avails regret? Regret cannot recall the dead, and as for me, I'll stand

> 'As if a man were author of himself,
> And knew no other kin.'

Hark! what's that?"

The loud rattle of carriage wheels, followed by a louder rat-tat at the door.

A moment later, and Brown announces, "Miss Trevor." The quick, light step of an elastic foot, the rustle of a woman's dress is heard, and Clara Trevor stands in the doorway.

The cynic, who a moment ago resolved to stand henceforth alone—the man whose dreary home had never been illumined by the light of a woman's smile, or made glad by the music of a woman's voice—stands spellbound as the apparition of the lost love of his youth starts into life again before him.

The girl had bounded forward, as if about to spring into the room, but paused and stood upon the threshold irresolute, as if uncertain of her welcome.

Her little sealskin hat had fallen from her head, her beautiful hair, released at that very moment from its confines, fell in thick flakes of burnished gold down her shoulders and below her waist, over a rough cloak or coat of fulvous vecuna, on the right arm of which she wore a large black band of crape. Her cheeks were suffused with blushes, her eyes were fixed full on him, as if timidly appealing.

He looked at her and through her, to years gone by, but stood still and spoke not.

She trembled and turned pale as death.

At last he extended his arms, and then, with a great tremor in his voice, as if in a dream, he uttered one word, and only one—it was "Maria!"

She understood the meaning and the memory, and ere the sound had faded from his lips she lay sobbing on his breast.

He caressed and soothed her. Then he said—"You know me?"

"Know you?" she answered, smiling through her tears, "I should have known you anywhere from mamma's description. She has told me of you so often that I feel as if I had known you all my life."

"You have your mother's eyes, your mother's smile, your mother's voice, child," he replied, gravely. Then, ringing the bell, he desired the servant to show the girl to her room.

While she is taking off her wraps above let me endeavour to describe the man in the room below.

He was about forty-five, but might have passed for ten years younger. Tall, straight as a dart, rather slender, hair of deep brown, a little streaked with grey at the temples, a massive brow, piercing grey eyes, a straight Grecian nose, oval face, mouth firm, almost severe. He had a somewhat repellant demeanour to strangers or intruders—a sort of "stand off" air—but to those who knew him and esteemed him, whether in the theatre or in society, he was both engaging and complaisant. He had literary tastes, wielded a facile and a fertile pen, was an admirable and accomplished actor and a great stage manager, and he knew it; so did everyone for that matter.

His whole career had been one social and artistic triumph, and yet he thought, on this particular night — yes — he — whatever he thought, his speculations were cut short by the return of his *protégée*.

Truly she made a charming picture, with her black cashmere dress, fastened up to the throat, with its plain bands of white at the neck and wrists, and a jet buckle at the slender waist. This simple costume displayed to rare advantage the graceful curves and exquisite undulations of her supple and beautiful figure.

She took the head of the table, as if she had been accustomed to it.

It seemed as if it really were as she had said—that she had known him all her life; and, for his part, he felt as if he had taken up some link in his past existence that had been lost ever so long ago.

After supper he opened his cigar-case and said —

"May I?"

"Certainly," she replied, "if I may light it for you. I always lighted papa's."

A slight cloud came over his brow. He hesitated a moment, and then said —

"Very well, you shall light mine if you will call me papa."

"May I?" she inquired, shyly.

"Yes," he answered; "and I will call you Clara."

They chatted away until he had finished his cigar. Then he rang the bell, and said — "To-morrow you shall do as you please, but I must be master to-night. You had better go to bed, child."

"You forget; you promised to call me Clara, papa."

"Well, Clara, then. God bless you, Clara."

And he kissed her, as her father might have done, as he bade her good-night.

When she reached her room (his chamber that was) she heard the moaning of the wind soughing round the gables of the old house. Save for this gruesome sound, all was still. The theatre was over long ago, and the heart of the city was at rest.

From afar, through the stillness of the night, came the shriek of the steam whistle and the throbbing of the engine, as the iron horse ploughed his way through the snow up to the bleak North.

The great bell of the minster tolled the midnight hour. The sound vibrated through the house, which it filled with a strange, weird music; then each church tower in the city rang out its answer, and ere the melody had melted into morning she lay sleeping with a smile upon her lips.

Meanwhile the lonely man below still sat reading the faces in the fire.

At last he started up, ejaculating sadly and bitterly—" And she might have been my child!"

Passing forth, he paused upon the landing while he called for his valet.

" Have you taken those rooms for Miss Trevor?" he inquired.

" No, sir; it was too late."

" Very well, then; I've altered my mind,

and you needn't trouble Mrs. Macnamara. Good-night."

" Good-night, sir."

And with that Fairfax entered the Ghost Room.

A strange eerie place it was; so, in fact, was the theatre itself. It was built amidst the ruins of an ancient convent, many of the walls of which had been utilized in the construction. The pit was laid over the oldest Norman arch in England, and in excavating the "well" of the stage a subterranean passage had been discovered which communicated with the abbey on the other side the river's bank.

From time immemorial the legend of "The White Ladye" had impermeated the place. It was an all too common story of the Dark Ages. A poor nun, who had been faithless to her vows, had been buried alive with her baby in a niche within those gloomy walls.

There was not a servant about the theatre who was not prepared to swear that he or she had seen at some time or other the apparition of " The White Ladye" in or about, going into, or coming out of, the " Ghost " Room.

Leigh, the London manager, an old chum of Fairfax's, slept there one night. He declared that at six o'clock in the morning, in the open day, with the summer sun streaming through the window, he awoke and saw a beautiful young woman in a nun's habit, with a baby in her arms, standing at the foot of his bed; that he got up to speak to her; that she disappeared through a recess, which he opened, and found to be a false cupboard, merely masking a niche in the old convent wall. Whether this was an hallucination or not, it is certain that, although he had accepted an invitation to remain for a week, Leigh precipitately left Rosemount the very next morning.

The wealth of the Indies would not have tempted Mrs. Brown to have slept a single night in the haunted chamber, and whenever that estimable woman arranged the room she always had Emma, the housemaid, to assist her, and Brown within hail.

Fairfax, however, did not believe in ghosts; he used to say he had seen too many of them —from "The Bleeding Nun" and "The Castle Spectre" up to "The Corsican Brothers."

Yet, sceptic as he was, that night Frank Fairfax saw, or perhaps he only dreamt that he saw, a ghost!

As he laid his head upon the pillow, fixing his eyes upon the fading fire, which filled the room with a dim, mystic light, the face which had haunted him all through the night emerged from the embers and grew and grew until it took the shadowy semblance of a fair woman in white, with bunches of transparent black about her lovely shoulders; a large fleecy hat, with gauze-like ribbons, thin as a spider's web, hung from her slender wrist; thick, long flakes of fair hair streamed down her shoulders, around her fair head was a golden nimbus, beneath which her large dark eyes shone like stars.

The shadow glided towards him, and he faced *it* without fear. *It* placed its arms around his neck, and pushed the hair from his brow, and kissed him, and murmured in a low, soft voice —

"Love her, Frank dear, love her!"

Then he made answer —

"Oh! my love, my lost love! I will be a father to her for your dear sake!"

Whereupon "The White Ladye" smiled with a radiant smile, and kept watch over his pillow while he slept, and chased the evil spirits of the night away.

BOOK THE FIRST.

CHAPTER I.

LOVE, LORD OF ALL.

" Love lacked a dwelling, and made him her place."

* * * * *

" She lifted up her eyes
And loved him with that love which was her doom."

THREE years had passed rapidly away since Clara Trevor's advent at Rosemount—three years of happiness for Fairfax and his adopted daughter—who had become light, life, air, and sunshine to him. For those three years he had been brighter and happier than he had ever been since that day on the Calton so long ago.

Had she been his own flesh and blood she could not have been nearer or dearer to him. As for her, she adored the very ground on which he walked.

It was a blessed night for both when that train from the north brought the orphan girl to the theatre house at Rosemount.

Her mother had not overrated the girl's ability. In addition to the breeding and education of a gentlewoman, she had all the gifts requisite for her art. A magnificent physique, a wonderful voice, an emotional temperament, vivid imagination, acute sensibility, poetic fancy, a quick study, the natural instinct of rhythm, both of voice and motion, combined with industry, application, sincerity, earnestness, and power. Obviously time and opportunity were only needed to enable her to develop into a great actress.

By degrees, and with admirable tact, Fairfax advanced her step by step, until she had almost reached the topmost rung of the ladder. His perfect mastery of the grammar of the stage rendered him an invaluable preceptor, and she was an apt pupil.

Then her youth, her beauty (for she had ripened into a woman of surpassing loveliness), and her accomplishments combined not only to make her a valuable acquisition to the company, but a great popular favourite; indeed, she had already become the most successful leading lady known in the circuit since the days of the Siddons and the Jordan.

Her attraction was perhaps enhanced by her inaccessibility. No Infanta of Spain was ever more jealously guarded.

Her studies were all-engrossing, and when it is remembered that she roamed from night to night, from Lady Teazle to Lady Macbeth, from Beatrice to Rosalind, from Portia to Parthenia, it will be obvious that she had little leisure. Fairfax's society (of which she had a monopoly) was enough for her; then, besides the fascination of her beloved art, she had her books and her music.

In the theatre she was affable and complaisant, but not particularly cordial; indeed, the young men of the company complained that she was particularly cold. Notwithstanding her frigidity, they admired her—much as stars and comets are admired—at a distance.

Certain it was, that as yet no one had made the slightest impression on that virgin heart; as yet the steel had not been forged to strike fire from that beautiful but invulnerable bosom. The fuel was there, certainly—combustible enough, and needing but the Promethean spark to leap into life and burst into a flame; but as yet the hour and the man had not come.

Now, were I a woman, I could devote a chapter, or a series of chapters, to a diagnosis of this innocent young creature's hopes, fears, and aspirations, while as yet she moved " in maiden meditation, fancy free," but I have a queer old-fashioned notion that a young maid's heart is too sacred a thing to be laid on a dissecting table and exposed to the public view; besides which, and apart from the fact that I am not versed in the mysteries of the feminine mind, this is a story of incident, and not a psychological study of character. I can only therefore chronicle the fact that, up to this moment, Clara Trevor was heart-whole, that her soul was as transparently pure as her body was beautiful, that she was as cold as an icicle, and chaste as sweet Artemis herself; but for all that, the invincible Prince was coming from " over the hills, and far away." Yes! Eros, the omnipotent, was coming to claim his own.

The arrangements of the Circuit took the company from town to town—sometimes for a few nights, sometimes for a season. In those days important London combinations were not wont to travel, and wherever the Great Northern Company went their visit was the event of the year; indeed, they were always sure of a cordial welcome, both in the theatre and in society.

At the time about to be described they had returned to Rosemount for the winter season. The —th Lancers was a theatrical regiment. The officers dined early, came to the theatre nightly, and behaved, I am glad to say this, like gentlemen, for I am constrained to admit with regret that at that period the good breeding of the gallant defenders of their Queen and country was not the quality most conspicuous during their visits to the boxes of a country theatre, or for that matter to any other place of public resort.

Fairfax was fond of hunting; he was a capital horseman, and a welcome guest at every hunt breakfast, and at many a pleasant dinner afterwards. Clara was not only an accomplished horsewoman, but had become one of the most attractive features of every hunting field in the county.

Now, it so happened that one morning, blessed with "a southerly wind and a cloudy sky," the manager and his ward put in an appearance together at the Marquis of H—'s meet.

Leaving Clara outside the Castle, attended by the groom, Fairfax went into the breakfast-room to fetch her a cup of tea. As he was returning, whom should he encounter but the Marquis himself. He had been Lord Chamberlain, and had seen Frank act all his crack parts in town. The old gentleman accosted him with a cheery "good-morning," and then inquired —

"Where are you off to, Fairfax, with that cup of tea?"

"It's for my daughter, sir!"

"Nonsense! can't allow it; pray introduce

me to Miss Trevor, and let me take her in to my wife and daughters."

The introduction was made, and then the genial old gentleman said, "Come, Miss Trevor —

'Though grey
Do something mingle with our younger brown, yet ha' we
A brain that nourishes our nerves.'

"Just place your little hands on my shoulders, and I'll lift you from your saddle like a bird. Allow me;" and down she sprang with a joyous laugh.

"That's right," he continued; "now let's leave this dissipated young dog to his weed with the men yonder, while we have a cup of tea with my lady and the girls."

In due course Clara was introduced to the Marchioness and her daughters, Florence and Mary (two graceful and unaffected young ladies), who were as delighted with her as she was with them.

Presently the girls rode out together, greatly to the mortification of certain young gentlemen who aspired to be their several escorts.

All the officers of the —th were there in full force. Two of these young fellows were distinguished beyond all the rest by their thoroughly good form, as well as by their good looks, and they sat their horses as if they had been born on their backs.

One of them had dark brown curling hair flecked with gold, an oval face, and deep blue eyes; he was broad-chested, slender-loined, and tiger-backed. The other was slighter, fairer, with sunny hair and laughing hazel eyes. Neither of them could have been less than twenty-one or more than five-and-twenty. When they saw the ladies the young men took off their hats and bowed. The girls, except Clara (who remained immovable), blushed and bowed again.

The darker of the two men looked at her for a moment; their eyes met; she flushed.

He bent to the saddle bow as he instinctively lifted his hat and gave his horse the spur. Florence looked rather astonished at this pantomime, and inquired —

"Do you know those men?"

"No, I do not," responded Clara.

"H'm," replied the girl, rather dubiously; "they are people of good family, though at present they are only ensigns in the Lancers quartered at Rosemount."

"By-the-bye, they are great play-goers. Talking at dinner the other day about you and Mr. Fairfax, they said they were delighted with your 'Beatrice' and charmed with his 'Benedict.' The fair boy, Mr. Armitage, admires you especially."

"Oh! indeed! and the other—the one with the dark hair?"

"Oh! his name is Herbert, but the men never call him by that name."

"Indeed!"

"No; papa says they always call him"

—and she hesitated a little—"'Handsome Jack.'"

"Handsome Jack!" echoed Clara.

"Yes; don't you think him handsome?" both the girls inquired.

"No, I don't," said Clara, very decidedly.

The conversation terminated abruptly, for the sly puss gave her horse the heel and sent him caracoling round.

After this the girls were all a little *gêné*. There's nothing, however, like the sound of horse and hound to "drive dull care away." Their youth, high spirits, the fine weather, the sound of the huntsman's horn, the crack of the whip, the baying of the hounds, and the cry of "Tally-ho! hark forward! tantivy!" set their blood flowing like quicksilver; so, giving their horses their heads, off they went with a burst, helter-skelter after the hounds.

Nothing stopped these young Amazons. The men were all good horsemen, but I think considerations of courtesy induced them to yield the lead to the ladies.

It was a pleasant, quick run for everybody, even for the fox, for he was run to cover, and they lost scent in less than three hours. Clara, for one, was glad that poor Reynard had escaped.

Returning from the hunt with her young friends, she found that they had read "Romeo and Juliet," and had got the Bard upon the brain.

Some charades and amateur performances had been given at the Castle, and among other selections the ball-room and the balcony scenes from "Romeo and Juliet" were presented. Florence had played Juliet, Mary the Nurse; "Handsome Jack," as he was called, and his friend Armitage, had played Romeo and Mercutio—and played them divinely—so at least the girls said.

On the other side of the field the two young men, having got the Marquis to introduce them, had declared to Fairfax that they also were "death" on Romeo and Mercutio.

"We oft rub shoulders with Fate as she hurries past," and thus the meet at H— Castle affected the lives of all those more or less connected with this veracious history.

As for Lady Florence and Lady Mary, in the fulness of time, the one became a countess, the other a marchioness; and I am under the impression they also became mothers of a race of earls and marquises and other such superior people.

It is more than likely, however, if Jack Herbert or Harry Armitage had had the pluck to pop the question that morning, the future peeresses would have chanced "the life to come" for the sake of becoming in the present Lady Florence Herbert and Lady Mary Armitage, in which case this story would have remained untold.

Whatever amount of courage the lads possessed, they evidently had not the inclination to try the experiment just then, for they rode back towards Rosemount with Fairfax, who, on Clara's approach, introduced them both to her.

The young fellows were most deferential and ingratiating, and endeavoured to render themselves particularly agreeable to the young lady, but she was very cold and reserved, and kept close to Fairfax's side. Perhaps he was not displeased at this, for he wanted to keep his darling to himself as long as he could.

When they reached the little house at the theatre, the groom came to help Clara dismount, but Herbert anticipated him, and was by her side like a flash of lightning.

Before she knew how it was done, her hands were on his shoulders, his arms were around her waist, and a strange thrill went coursing through her every vein.

As she alighted they looked once more full in each other's eyes. He lifted his hat, she bowed in return, then pulling up her habit she rapidly entered the house.

Fairfax was, at that moment, occupied with Armitage making an engagement to dine at the mess the following week. Herbert remounted; the gentlemen shook hands and parted with mutual expressions of good-will.

As they rode away Armitage said —

"What do you think of her, Jack?"

"I think she rides to hounds capitally, is a charming actress, and altogether about the most beautiful girl I ever saw."

"Ah! well, that's good enough."

"Good enough for what?" said Herbert curtly, and even sternly.

"Why, for Mrs. Herbert."

"Quite, if she saw it and I saw it from that point of view, but I don't suppose she does. Fairfax is wealthy—she is his heiress—besides which she's bound to make her fortune on the stage, while I—well! I'm too poor, and too proud to live upon my wife. Don't you remember the story of the singing woman who married a marquis—a miserable creature. After paying his gambling debts half a dozen times she divorced him. Plucking a diamond necklace, worth a king's ransom, from her neck, she threw it in the fellow's face, as she said, 'Take that! For that and the like of it you sold yourself to slavery; with it I buy my liberty. Begone! *Lâche!*'

"My God! imagine any woman ever having the chance of saying that or anything like it to Jack Herbert! Enough. Say no more about it, Hal," and they set spurs to their horses.

And Clara?

She was unusually quiet at dinner, and though she piled Fairfax's plate with dainties, scarcely tasted food herself.

"What's the matter my darling?" he enquired, as he came and placed his arms tenderly around her.

Ah! his gentle caresses did not send the hot blood to her heart like yonder man's simple touch.

She merely murmured languidly —

"Nothing, papa! only I'm rather tired, and my head aches a little, that's all. If you don't mind I'll lie down for an hour or two. I shall be better by-and-bye," and so she left him to his *Times*, his claret, and his after-dinner cigar.

Poor girl! "The very pin of her heart was cleft with the blind bow-boy's butt shaft."

When she looked into John Herbert's eyes, quick and fleeting as was the glance, she saw her fate lay mirrored there.

Her hour had come—the hour which comes to every man and every maid, sooner or later.

CHAPTER II.

ROMEO AND JULIET.

"For never was a story of more woe
Than this of Juliet and her Romeo."

A FORTNIGHT after the meet at H— orders came down from the Horse Guards for the —th Lancers to put themselves in marching order and to be prepared to start at a week's notice for Egypt, where the war in the Soudan was then raging.

Then came a succession of farewell dinners and dances. To give additional *éclat* to the occasion, Herbert and Armitage induced Fairfax to let them have the theatre for an amateur performance of " Romeo and Juliet" by the men of the regiment.

Now, this affair nearly came to grief through the unexpected and apparently inexplicable absence from the rehearsal of the chaplain of the regiment, the Honourable and Reverend Philip Blake, of Castle Blake, County Galway, commonly called " Fighting Phil."

Dear old Phil was as fine a fellow as ever stood in shoe-leather (and he stood six feet without his shoes), but he ought to have been a barrister, a soldier, an actor—anything but a parson.

He was dying to distinguish himself as Friar Lawrence.

Barring the brogue, he spoke the lines admirably, and had a fair idea of the parts, thanks to the capital coaching of Joe Boanergus, Fairfax's " heavy man," who came to look after the preliminary rehearsals.

Altogether a remarkable person was Joe, with his bullet-head, his black hair cropped to the poll, his keen, glittering eyes, his pale face, his close-shaven blue-black beard, and his mouth with the teeth of a badger and the jaw of a bulldog. A heavy swell, too, was he, in his stylish great coat with sealskin collar and cuffs, his white silk muffler tied carelessly round his neck, his cloth boots tipped with patent leather, his malacca cane, silver-topped, his kid gloves, and his hat curled up at the brim.

"Fighting Phil" didn't come to the second rehearsal, whereupon Joe kicked up a row and dismissed the people.

That afternoon "Phil" turned up at the theatre house, and was shown into the manager's den, where presently Frank Fairfax joined him.

Frank went in "like a lion," but after five minutes' jaw came out "like a lamb."

The parson stayed to dinner, and assisted in spoiling a leg of Welsh mutton, and also assisted in polishing off a couple of bottles of Fairfax's famous old port, before he returned to quarters.

Next day Boanergus rehearsed the Friar himself, so that difficulty was got over.

It was a crying grievance to Phil, however, that pressure had been brought to bear to induce him to throw up the part.

This was how it happened:—

The Dean (a pottering old idiot, who was always poking his nose into other people's business) got wind, through some of the boys who were dining at the Deanery, of Phil's intention, so this asinine pillar of the Church thought it incumbent on him to warn Blake of the consequences of such a breach of decorum —consequences which he alleged would be serious, perhaps fatal to his professional advancement.

"Sure, boys," said Phil, "I meant to have put myself behind a magnificent 'bird.' Then, with a bald wig and 'Mr. Anon' in the playbill, who the devil would have recognized Phil Blake?"

Clara knew that so long as her secret was her own she was safe; hence to the dove's innocence she added a little of the serpent's wisdom, and when not engaged in the business of the scene she was distantly courteous to Herbert, and no more.

Once on the stage, her eyes, her looks, her tremulous and pathetic utterance of the Veronean maiden's ecstatic but unhappy love were all but too eloquent tell-tales.

Herbert could not understand how it was possible she could grow hot and cold in the same breath; how she could fix her eyes upon him at their first meeting in the ballroom, as if she were spellbound; how she could look down upon him from the balcony as if she were about to leap into his arms or draw him up to hers; how she could cling to him with convulsive ardour at their last fatal parting, and yet, a moment after, could be frigid as an iceberg. Although *he* couldn't understand these strange phenomena, Fairfax knew the symptoms only too well. Seeing the estrangement increase between the young people, he was actually drawn towards Herbert, who was so modest, so unpretentious, so manly, that at last Frank's heart went out to him. "If they love each other," he growled to himself, "why, they do, and there's an end of it; but it's a pity such a fine fellow should go to cut a throat or have his own cut for three half-crowns a day when he could do so much better at home."

At length came the eventful night. All the men turned up in a dreadful state of nervousness, and had it not been for Blake I don't know what would have become of them. He buzzed about from dressing-place to dressing-place, laughing and joking here, there, and everywhere. His laughter was contagious, and the boys began to laugh a little themselves. Then he had some tea brought in, and gradually they began to forget, for a moment at least, the very existence of nerves.

"Shure, boys," said he, "I'm here to tache you how to behave yourselves to the girls, and especially to look after that thief of a Romeo, who goes about jumping over walls, climbing balconies, and killing people on the slightest provocation.

"By my honor, that friar was a sinsible owld man, and knew what he was about when he said —

"'For by your laves you shall not stay alone
Till holy Church incorporate two in one.'

"Besides, who knows but you might be afther mateing wid an accident—tumbling down one of the holes in that murthering stage; and then where would you be without the parson?

"Wherever the regiment is there am I, so long as a rag of the flag hangs together."

Of course, it goes without saying that there was an enormous house. Friends are always willing to come to see fellows make fools of themselves; in fact, it is one of those privileges of which friendship steadfastly avails itself. But the men of the —th were not such sticks as amateurs usually are; most of them certainly looked guys in their mediæval costumes, while, as for their riding rods of legs!— It is a singular thing that cavalry officers never have legs; I suppose it is a qualification for that branch of the service. It is certain, however, there was only one pair of legs in the regiment, and those were Romeo's. Well, as soon as he had made his first plunge, and surmounted his nervousness, he spoke like a Christian, moved like a man and a gentleman; nay, had some idea of the rhythmical intonation of the verse. He looked a picture; and his voice—ah! he always had a voice that went straight to every heart. Fairfax, who was hard to please, sat in his box holding a post-mortem examination on everything and everybody.

At the end of the Balcony Scene he exclaimed —

"By Jove! the boy will make an actor."

And Clara! Well, it was conceded on all hands that her Juliet was not a transformation—it was a transfiguration; all hearts went out to her, and she struck the chords of every emotion, whether she melted into pathos, rose to passion, or sank into despair.

Herbert could never surely have escaped the universal contagion had not his poverty and his pride rendered him invulnerable. "In the very torrent and tempest" of his passion —even while they were both quivering in the ecstasy of simulated love—each felt an insuperable barrier of pride arise like a pillar of ice between them.

When the curtain fell and they came forth to receive the congratulations of their friends, amidst the flowers at their feet lay a golden laurel wreath, which Romeo lifted from the stage and placed upon Juliet's head.

Could he or she, amidst that whirlwind of excitement, have caught a glimpse of the pale, anguished face of poor little Lady Florence, who had prepared the wreath for him, and now saw "her Romeo" place it on the head of her rival, Juliet, it would surely have a little dashed their triumph.

As they left the stage, Herbert said —
"Good-bye, Miss Trevor; thanks, a thousand and a thousand times, for your endurance of my crude efforts. With such a Juliet to inspire me I ought to have done better; believe, however, I have done my best. Now, once more thanks, and farewell."

He pressed her hand, and was gone ere she could speak.

For a moment she was silent, then, waking as if from a dream, she turned wearily towards her dressing-room, murmuring to herself the lines she had heard him speak the moment immediately preceding her first entrance. The words are not Shakespere's, but Garrick's, yet, despite the cant of the purists, they are quite good enough to be the poet's own: 'tis thus they run:—

> " 'Twas through my eyes the shaft empierced my heart,
> Chance gave the wound which time can never heal.
> No star befriends me.
> " To each sad night succeeds a dismal morrow,
> And still 'tis hopeless love and endless sorrow."

Poor Clara! that was the burden of her song for many a weary day and many a sleepless night to come.

CHAPTER III.

"THE GIRLS THEY LEFT BEHIND THEM."

"Good-bye, sweetheart, good-bye."

WHEN Phil Blake and his young friends got to town he joined his family in Kennington Park Terrace, while Armitage went to his father's house at South Kensington, and Herbert put up at the Hummums.

The day after their arrival Hal asked his comrades to dinner at Hollywood Lodge.

The boy's mother was dead; his father, an Alderman of the City of London, a wealthy merchant, and an M.P. to boot, was a blatant, purse-proud, well-meaning old Philistine, with not one aspiration in common with his son.

Both Phil and Herbert tried to make themselves agreeable, but despite the sumptuous repast the attempt was a failure. They made no secret of their poverty, and the Alderman boasted continually of his wealth. He opened fire by suggesting that they should make the most of the spread and the wine.

"Tuck in, my lads," said he; "you don't get a feed like this every day."

Phil flushed up to his eyes, and gasped, but ultimately gulped down his indignation with a glass of Madeira. Herbert was rather amused, but poor Hal with difficulty restrained his annoyance and mortification.

"I dessay you wouldn't think it," said the Alderman, "but that salmon cost me five shillings a pound!"

"In that case, I'll trouble you for another half-pound," said Phil, gravely.

"Is that the way you eat salmon in Ireland?" enquired the Alderman.

"No, sir; we eat herrings there, and give the salmon to the peasants and the pigs!"

"Sir-er!" exclaimed the Alderman.

"Beg pardon. When I spoke of pigs I didn't mean to be personal," said Blake.

Herbert nearly barked Phil's shins under the table, and he "dried up" for a time. Meanwhile poor Hal thought —

"If they've got to this with the fish what will it be by-and-bye?"

When they reached the dessert the Alderman was more blatant that ever, but Phil kept pace with his host, and never flinched from his bottle until they were both well under weigh.

Meanwhile the two young men sat on thorns, and while their elders were pegging away at the port they stuck to the claret.

"That's Château Margaux, my boys," said the Alderman. "A guinea and a half a bottle. You're not likely to get much of that in Egypt. Have another glass of port, parson? It's better than the black strap you get at your mess, I'll be bound. What do you think of it?"

"H'm! Pretty good for Kensington," said Blake, "but not what we are accustomed to in Galway."

"Galway be d—d! Poor poverty-stricken, priest-ridden country, where the people live on 'potatoes and point,' and not much of that. That port, sir, cost me thirty-six pounds a dozen—that's sixty shillings a bottle. Sixty shillings, sir; think of that!"

"Ah!" said Blake reflectively, "let me see. Twelve glasses to the bottle. Pass the decanter, Alderman, and I'll take another crown's worth."

"Parson," said the Alderman, "it strikes me very forcibly you wouldn't put it down so easily if you had to pay for it."

"It strikes me very forcibly," replied Phil,

"I should put it down much easier, for I shouldn't have an Alderman of the City of London to take the trouble to keep count of the number of glasses I take."

"Counting, sir," roared the Alderman. "Counting is my business. I've made that boy's fortune by counting. I'll bet you a thousand pounds to a shilling that I count more thousands of pounds than you can count sovereigns!"

"I can't undertake to do that," responded the Parson with grim pleasantry, "because I've only got one in the world; but I bet you a sovereign to a tenpenny nail that I put down a sovereign for every idea you've got in your head, Mr. Armitage," and he laid the sovereign down on the table.

"Tell 'ee what it is, young jackanapes," growled the Alderman to Hal, "if you've brought these fellows here only to insult your father, the sooner they are out of this the better."

So saying he staggered over to the bell, and when the butler came he said —

"'Awkins, you can show these gents the other side of the door; and that puppy of mine can go with 'em if he likes."

Out went the guests without further ceremony. When they got outside Herbert said —

"Phil! how could you? Only see what you have let poor Hal in for."

"By my honour I'm sorry that I forgot myself, for your sake, dear boy, for whatever you're father is you're a gentleman; but you see, I'm a Blake of Galway, and I'm not accustomed to take a blow without giving a thrust.

"Come and dine with me, boys, before we leave town. I can't give you port at sixty bob a bottle, but I'll give you a leg of Welsh mutton, a glass of claret, a jug of punch, and a *cead mihlle fealtha*, and I'll introduce you to the best wife and daughter in the world.

Now mind, the day after to-morrow, six o'clock sharp, 59, Kennington Park Terrace. That's an appointment."

So the friends shook hands and parted, leaving poor Hal to confront the Alderman's wrath. Fortunately, when the boy got back, the stern parent had returned to his potations with such a will that he was quite oblivious and had to be helped to bed, and was conscious the next morning of nothing worse than a headache, and an indistinct recollection of having had a slight difference of opinion with Hal's friends.

Next day Herbert went down to Cambridge, where he found his father broken down by chronic bronchitis. The flat, marshy neighbourhood of the dear old place, which was associated with the lad's happiest days, had aggravated the malady, and winter after winter the poor gentleman got worse.

Mrs. Herbert, a charming old lady, took

the first opportunity, when they were alone, to tell Jack that she thought his father was getting near the end of his journey.

The doctor who came to dine with them had known Herbert from boyhood, and as they walked to the "Bull" together, after dinner, said to him —

"Jack, I'm afraid it's a bad look out for your mother. We are going to have an unusually severe winter, and if your father doesn't get away to Cannes, or Nice, or somewhere in the Riviera, he's a doomed man."

Happily the poor gentleman himself had no idea that the end was so near. So when they parted he was elate, and confident, and full of plans for the future. Not so Herbert and his mother.

"John," said she, "for your poor mother's sake, be careful of your precious life. I fear soon you will be all I shall have left in the world."

"Mother," he replied, "Heaven will protect me for your sake. You'll let me know if the worst should happen?"

"Be sure of that. God bless you, my boy," and so they parted.

On his return to the Hummums, Herbert found a note from Phil Blake, reminding him of their appointment; and before six o'clock Harry Armitage called and bowled him down to Kennington in the Alderman's brougham.

Phil, who was usually rather careless in his costume, was on this occasion "got up regardless," more, it must be said, in honour of his womenkind than his young comrades. He came forward with a genial welcome, and after a minute's chat he said —

"Now, boys, let me introduce you to my wife and daughter—here they are," and the two ladies entered the room.

"Gabrielle, my dear—Caroline, my love,"

said he, "let me introduce to you my dearest friends, John Herbert and Harry Armitage."

Mrs. Blake and her daughter came forward, and without fuss or the pretence of ceremony, made the young fellows welcome, and in five minutes they were at home.

The two ladies appeared to be younger and elder sister—no more.

The younger was evidently about eighteen; the elder did not look a day more than thirty, thought it is obvious she must have been a little older to be the mother of such a daughter.

They had just returned from Paris, where they had lived for the past two years. Both were dressed exactly alike, in simple gowns of purple cashmere, high to the throat, falling closely to the figure, merely relieved by a plain white collar and cuffs, and a single band of ribbon, with a dainty little gold buckle at the waist, and a small enamelled brooch at the throat. Each had one rich crimson rose placed amidst the abundant tresses, which coiled closely to the head, and were fastened in a Grecian knot behind.

Although their features were cast in the same mould, they were as different as day and night in complexion. Madame's hair was of a rich reddish bronze; Caroline's was like her father's, black as night, or rather of the transparent blue black which takes so many shades in the sunlight.

The mother's head and face were pure Greek—low brow, straight eyebrows, grey eyes, oval face, short lips, beautiful teeth, with the bloom of the peach upon her cheeks, and the slightest suspicion of its down upon her lip.

Caroline inherited all the beauty of her mother, commingled with the rich Iberian blood of the Blakes. Wonderful eyes of Irish blue, with great long curled "lashes," a skin transparent as alabaster, beneath which the colour came and went as the golden sunshine flickers through the clouds on a September morning.

Mrs. Blake was a woman of remarkable accomplishments, an admirable musician, both vocal and instrumental, a wonderful linguist, an expert needlewoman, and a charming artist in water-colours.

To all her mother's gifts Caroline added strong dramatic instincts, a taste fostered by her Parisian friends, who, after the fashion of their country, went to the play almost nightly, taking the girl and her mother with them. Two or three nights every week they went to the Français, and thus became familiarized not only with the best French dramatic literature and the admirable acting of the accomplished comedians of the "House of Molière," but more especially with the performances of the distinguished actress whose star was then at its zenith.

It was not surprising, therefore, that the

girl devoured every detail of the performance of " Romeo and Juliet," which was related at length by Armitage for the delectation of her mother and herself, listening with especial interest to Hal's description of " the beautiful Miss Trevor."

Once she asked Herbert—" Do you think her beautiful, Mr. Herbert ? "

Herbert replied—" Beauty is a matter of taste, Miss Blake. Miss Trevor is certainly very beautiful, but I think I have seen someone who more thoroughly realizes my idea of beauty."

At this moment, with the ready tact of a mother, and an Irishwoman, Mrs. Blake changed the subject ; she proposed some music, and they adjourned to the piano. Hal thought he had never heard such music in his life. Madame's voice, which was a ripe mezzo-soprano, paled before her daughter's, which had a wonderful range, being especially rich in the lower notes.

Caroline sang to Madame's accompaniment, Madame sang to hers, then they sang and played together. They sang Moore's melodies, they sang chansonettes and arias, and then, to the astonishment of the young men, Caroline produced her violin, on which she played a fantasia on " The Last Rose of Summer " with a fervour and feeling which enchanted them.

Phil cut in and said—" Now, boys, I'll let you have an Irish song that'll go with the punch. Gabrielle, my darling, give us the ' Cruiskeen Lawn ' ; " and he sang it with a life and go that was irresistible. Hal contributed his mite with the last music hall absurdity, which set everybody off laughing.

Then Phil called on Herbert, who tried to excuse himself. " I only know one ballad," he said, " and as unfortunately I cannot play my own accompaniment, 'tis useless for me to try it."

" Ah, g'long—you good men are so modest; sure Sims Reeves isn't in it with you. And haven't I accompanied you in it a thousand times? So look out, bright chanticleer—here goes!" And he struck up " Good-bye, sweetheart, good-bye," while Herbert, in a rich baritone, sang the simple and touching melody.

The pleasantest evening must come to an end, so at last the young fellows bade their friends good-night, having arranged to meet at the Lyceum the following evening.

When they were seated in the brougham Hal said —

" Isn't she an angel, Jack?"

" She is charming."

" Charming! She's the most beautiful creature on the face of God's earth; and if ever I live to come back—"

" Well, if ever you do ? "

" You'll see."

" That's right, old man. Now give us a light."

Then they subsided into silence until Hal dropped Jack at " The Hummums."

The following evening the lads met Phil and the ladies at the Lyceum. The play was " Much Ado About Nothing," a sumptuous spectacle which they followed with eager interest.

Phil sat in the centre, with Mrs. Blake on his left hand and Caroline on his right. Hal was next to Caroline, and did his utmost to make himself agreeable, but evidently without much success, for the young lady replied only in monosyllables, and appeared very *distraite*. Herbert was next to Mrs. Blake, who rattled away at every interval with all the charm and vivacity of her race ; but, strange to say, Herbert was not particularly responsive, so

Phil, Mrs. Blake, and Hal had the burden of the talk to themselves.

When the performance was over, Phil and the ladies returned to Kennington, and Herbert and Hal strolled over to E.'s to have some supper, and there, I fear, they had more wine than was good for them.

Hal was effusive and confidential. He had been to see Phil that morning, and had obtained permission (provided he could obtain his father's consent) to pay his addresses to Miss Blake on his return from Egypt, but it was understood that the matter was to remain in abeyance until then.

Herbert received this communication almost in silence. He merely said —

"I hope you will be happy, Hal. If she loves you, you are sure to be happy."

"*If* she loves me? She's bound to love me, Jack. There's no other fellow in the way—if there were, by —! I'd shoot him. And if the governor isn't a swell, he'll cut up for half a million; and I'm not such a bad sort, you know."

"Say no more, old fellow, say no more; and let us hope it'll all turn out as you wish."

"That's right, Jack; you're the best fellow in the world, and I hope you'll be happy with Clara Trevor one of these fine days."

"I don't think that is likely," coldly replied Herbert.

At this moment a choir of boys struck up an old madrigal; it was one that Herbert's mother had sung to him as a child. Apart from this it was a strain of heavenly music, and melted their hearts into tenderness and love. They hugged each other—for they were only lads; then they cried and swore eternal friendship.

Next morning a vast concourse of people assembled on Waterloo Bridge, and crowded the road down to the station gates to see the troops march past on their way to Portsmouth.

The sun was high in heaven, banners waving, band playing, and the crowd shouting.

When Herbert and Armitage, at the head of their detachment, reached the Surrey side of the bridge a well-known voice rang out above the rest —

"More power to ye, boys; till Portsmouth, good-bye!"

Looking to the right they saw Phil, Mrs. Blake, and Caroline standing in the balcony of one of the first houses on the terrace. They saluted, and the ladies waved their handkerchiefs. A mist of tears clouded bright eyes and welled forth from brave hearts, while high above the din the noon-tide hour rang out from St. Paul's, and from every church tower the silvery chimes made joyous answer.

The band struck up "The girl I left behind

me;" and amidst the waving of hats and handkerchiefs, the roar of the multitude, the braying of the band, and the clangour of the bells, Herbert and Armitage passed forth to their last campaign.

BOOK THE SECOND.

ROBERT PENARVON'S NARRATIVE.

CHAPTER I.

ORESTES AND PYLADES (A RETROSPECT).

"Oh! Pylades, what is life without a friend?"

I, ROBERT PENARVON, who tell this story, will say as little about myself or my antecedents as possible, save to indicate my connection with the incidents hereafter related.

Of course everybody knows the Penarvons, of Penarvon Grange, Cornwall.

I was called Robert, after my grandfather,

who I have heard was a cranky, crusty, cruel old man.

His eldest son, Roland, my father, was a captain in the East India Company's service, and when he was home on leave, after a long spell in the East, he ran away with the daughter of one of my grandfather's tenants, and married her.

Grandfather would have forgiven father for running away with my mother, but for making her his wife he was never forgiven.

The property was not entailed, so the whole estate, real and personal, was bequeathed to father's younger brother, Stephen, who, after grandfather's death, married the cook, by whom he had a numerous family of clodhoppers, and that is all I know, or ever cared to learn, about them or theirs.

I was born in India, and my poor mother died the moment I saw the light. My father, stricken with a mortal malady, sold out, and returned to England.

In the course of time he put me to school at Clapham, where he took up his quarters, that he might see me as often as possible.

For the first two years he came for me regularly every Wednesday afternoon, and we used to take long rambles together over the beautiful heaths and moorlands in the neighbourhood, then uninvaded by jerry builders and railways.

Every Sunday, after midday, I was father's own boy until Monday morning.

Poor father! he was ill—very ill.

At last he was taken from me, and at twelve years of age I was left alone in the world. I was always a shy, awkward, taciturn lad, but I became more so than ever after father's death, and the bigger fellows were disposed to "put" on the "nigger," as they called me, because of my dark complexion and my being born in India.

Jim Bulstrode, a great hulking hobbledehoy, was the cock of the school, and he used to order us about like galley-slaves. Woe betide anyone who dared dispute his commands; it was a word and a blow, only, unfortunately for us little ones, the blow came first and the word after. There was only one lad in the school to whom Bulstrode gave a wide berth, a lad of about fifteen, who had only just joined us. He was very bright, very handsome, and very clever, but very proud and distant with us all. I think I can see him now, with his beautiful oval face, his open but imperious brow, crowned with clusters of dark brown curls flecked with gold, his dark eyebrows and long curled lashes veiling his great, dreamy, deep blue eyes; his straight, delicately-chiselled nose, his dimpled chin, and his firm-set mouth. A month after his arrival he stood at the head of the first class in every department.

M. Anatole de la Forge, our old French dancing master, who pronounced me an *imbecile,* declared that the new-comer danced like young Sylvain; while Sergeant Gribble, our old sword master, who had served in the Crimea, swore that his calisthenics were tip-top, that his broad-sword play was worthy of a Life Guardsman; and that in the grand salute and lightness of touch with the foils he was equal to Angelo or Charles Kean, the play actor, whom Gribble had once seen at the Princess's.

All this high falutin stuff would have turned an ordinary lad's head, but it fell like water off a duck's back from the young stranger.

How or where he learnt his lessons we never knew.

As a rule, during play time, he retired to some secluded corner and occupied himself with a pocket edition of Shakespere, which was his inseparable companion morning, noon, and night.

He seldom played with us, but when he did we found to our cost that he was the best cricketer, jumper, swimmer, and runner amongst us.

Besides these accomplishments he was master of another, of which we knew nothing till a certain memorable occasion, when he enlightened Bulstrode and the rest of us—more particularly Bulstrode.

The stranger's name was John Herbert, but no one ever took the liberty to accost him by his Christian name out of school. All the boys, except Bulstrode, called him " The Prince ; " he called him " The Cub "—not to his face though.

One night, after we had gone to bed, our tyrant routed me up, and ordered me to go and steal some King William pears, which grew in the garden beneath our window.

I fear I was not so loth to commit this petty larceny as I ought to have been. So when they lowered me down by a sheet I went to work with a will, clambered up the tree, had a jolly tuck in on my own account before

I descended with as many pears as I could carry in a pillow case.

When I began the job the moon shone as bright as noontide; before I had finished it was dark as pitch.

I alighted on *terra firma* safely enough, but I couldn't find the window, and went blundering about in the dark, until I fell head foremost into a cucumber frame, smashing the glass in every direction, breaking my nose, cutting my hands, and making a most diabolical row, which startled the whole house.

Cries of "Murder!" "Thieves!" &c., arose in every direction, and before I could extricate myself from the cucumbers, the Doctor's great beastly bull terrier, Pongo, had pinned me by my breeches, and when Joe, the gardener, pulled him off, the brute brought away something more than the seat of my trousers.

When I regained my feet I was confronted by the Doctor, with a blunderbuss as big as himself, the ushers with their rattans, the servants with lights.

A nice thing I had dropped in for! These pears were the Doctor's especial weakness.

It was rumoured that when they appeared at dessert, neither Mrs. Thorpe nor the Misses Thorpe, not even Aurelia, his especial favourite, ever presumed to look at them. When, therefore, he found that I had dared to lay felonious hands upon his treasures, his rage knew no bounds. The old brute offered to let me off if I would peach on my pals. Of course, an infamy like that was not to be thought of, so I was tried and convicted without benefit of jury, and there and then horsed upon Joseph's back twice up and down the dormitory, for the delectation of my brother culprits. Horsed did I say? I was almost flayed alive!

Next day we all had " tasks " (I have hated the name of Virgil ever since), and there was plenty of "clapper clawing" knocking about during those tasks, I promise you.

I soon learned the difference between success and failure. Had I succeeded in bringing back the pears in triumph I should have been a hero; having failed, I was a duffer. No word was bad enough for me.

"The Prince" didn't "chum" in the same dormitory with us, and he tried to pump me as to what had happened, but I wouldn't split, so he became more cold even than usual.

The next Wednesday, during our half-holiday, a council of war was held in the playground, and as a penance for my past offence Bulstrode ordered me to attempt the pear-tree again that very night. On my venturing to demur he threatened to thrash me within an inch of my life, and the beast was as good as his word, for he gave me a clout on the head which sent me to the other side of the yard. I was staggered for a moment, but recovering myself I rushed at him and did my little utmost to give as good as I took. I might as well have stood up against Jack Heenan or Ben Caunt. The fellow hit me wherever he liked. I was knocked about like a shuttlecock, and bruised and beaten into a jelly bag; in fact, I was nearly done for, when help came from an unexpected quarter.

"The Prince," who was reading his everlasting Shakespere and munching an orange at the other end of the playground, lounged leisurely up to the spot, and said quietly, but imperiously —

"Take your hands from the boy. Do you hear?"

Bulstrode opened his eyes in amazement.

"Were you speaking to me, you impudent cub?" he inquired.

"Yes, I was speaking to you," responded "The Prince;" "and what is more, Mr. Jowls, if you give me any of your lip I'll give you the soundest beating you ever had in your life."

With a howl of rage Bulstrode "went" for "The Prince," who, dexterously avoiding the blow, gave Master Jim a crack in the eye with the orange. Then, with the utmost composure, pocketing his Shakespere, he took off his jacket and turned up his shirt-sleeves. These precautions completed, he said with the utmost *sang froid* —

"Now, Master Jowls, I am going to astonish you," and he did astonish him and everybody else.

Boxing was the shining light this modest young gentleman had kept hidden under a bushel. His "science" was perfect, and I quite forgot my own licking in my admiration of the charmingly scientific manner in which he gave Bulstrode his "gruel."

After about ten minutes of it he threw up the sponge ignominiously, and left "The Prince" cock of the walk. Then, while the discomfited bully made the best of his way with a beautiful pair of black eyes to the pump, the boys carried the victor in triumph round the playground.

What marvel after this that Jack Herbert and I were friends and brothers!

Although barely three years older than myself, I looked up to him as my protector, and somehow he seemed to take the place of the father I had lost.

In his moments of confidence he informed me that he, like myself, was intended for the army, and that his father was a college tutor at Cambridge, poor as Job, and proud as Lucifer, and that poverty and pride ran in the blood of the Herberts.

For my part I hadn't much to boast of in the way of wealth; my small inheritance had, however, been judiciously invested by Mr. Stanton, our solicitor, to whom my father's affairs were confided, and who consented to act as trustee and executor.

Like myself, Jack had little taste for the military profession. Just before he came to Clapham he had been taken to see Phelps at Drury Lane; his *idée fixe* was to be an actor, a tragedian, but since his father would have none of it, and as he believed thoroughly in the Fifth Commandment, he made up his mind to yield obedience to the paternal wishes.

As soon as he took me under his protecting wing time passed pleasantly enough for me, and, indeed, for the other lads, since thenceforth the bold Bulstrode "let us severely alone."

My only bad times were the holidays, when every boy but me went home to his friends, and I was left alone, except, indeed, one never-to-be-forgotten Christmas, when Jack took me down to Cambridge with him. It was the bitterest winter known for years, but it was summer to me, rosy, golden summer.

The following Christmas was our last at

Clapham. We were both booked for Sandhurst, where he had to fight my battles as well as his own, which kept him pretty well occupied out of school hours.

After the usual course of "cram" we passed our "exams." in triumph; then, through the influence of one of his father's pupils, on the one hand, and Mr. Stanton on other, we were drafted, the one into the —th Lancers, the other into the Scots Greys.

Before we left Sandhurst Jack's dramatic proclivities asserted themselves. We had a play, or rather a part of a play—the third act of "Julius Cæsar," in which "The Prince" distinguished himself highly as Marc Antony, and I failed miserably in the "lean and hungry" Cassius.

At last came the time for us to part.

Next to father's death this was the greatest grief of my young life.

When we got to town Jack went one way and I another. It was a sad hour for both.

Our separation extended over a considerable period, during which we corresponded regularly. In all that time we had both been on active service in different parts of the globe.

Five years had elapsed since we parted at Sandhurst, and I was quartered at Sheffield when I received a telegram from Jack asking me if I would like to exchange into his regiment.

As if it were necessary to ask such a question! Of course, I jumped at the idea, and in less than a week afterwards the transfer was effected, and I was on my way to Portsmouth.

Before proceeding to the next chapter I may here remark that the principal events I am about to relate occurred mostly under my own eyes; and the connecting links are based upon such authentic information as to induce me to incorporate them bodily with this narrative.

CHAPTER II.

EN ROUTE TO THE EAST.

*" What envious streaks
Do lace the severing clouds in yonder East."*

UPON arriving at Portsmouth I was delighted to find myself once more with the friend of my boyhood—I may say my only friend. Jack was as pleased to see me as I was to see him. He introduced me to his comrades as *his* especial chum, and I made myself at home directly—more particularly with his most intimate friends, Phil Blake and Harry Armitage.

Some two or three days elapsed in getting

our stores and horses embarked. The very day after my arrival who should "turn up" at mess but Armitage's father.

The boy was an only child, and the old man softened at the thought of losing him for a time, perhaps for all time, so he came down and declared on to the Colonel, Herbert, and Phil Blake. At first Phil was cold and even arctic; presently, however, he relented, and then he and the old gentleman became inseparable.

A common tie united them.

Armitage was parting with his boy—Phil was leaving his loved ones behind.

The day before we sailed Mr. Armitage gave a dinner—a princely banquet—not to us five alone, but to all the regiment, from the men upwards. Even the band after they had played through our dinner had a sumptuous spread to themselves, and the band-master, Van Vort, an eccentric little foreigner (I never knew whether he was a Hollander, a Bavarian, or a Belgian, but he was a gentleman, I'm sure), was asked in to wine with us. By-and-bye he brought in a strange-looking musical instrument—a zither, I think, he called it—on which he played all kinds of strange tunes and weird fantasias.

Being, unfortunately, not a musician, I know not how to describe these things. I only know that the little man was a long time torturing and tuning his instrument, that he commenced with a dreamy Hungarian waltz which changed to " Juanita."

Presently he became as one inspired, his face and form betraying the strong emotion which thrilled his blood and brain, while he poured forth his soul through his finger-tips into the instrument, which throbbed, responsive to his touch, as if it were a human creature endowed with a seraphic voice which rose in a crescendo of heavenly music. The jubilate glided gradually into a pathetic minor, a soft liquid melody, compounded of native land, of home, and ingle neuk; of the soft soughing of the west wind; of rain-drops pattering softly on rustling leaves; of great rivers gently gliding to the sea; of plighted troths, of kisses, of blessings and farewells; of sighs, and sobs, and tears—" tears wrung from the depths of a divine despair"—when, lo! at the very moment when this " linked sweetness long drawn out" faded into "a sound so fine that nothing lived 'twixt it and silence," it swelled and swelled till it burst forth and filled the air like the last song of some poor dying bird rising to the empyrean and pouring out its heart, in its last agony before the gates of God!

No roaring of the loud-mouthed multitude could ever have rendered such eloquent homage to the genius of the musician as our tears and our silence, amidst which he rose and glided forth pale and speechless as a ghost.

For a while we remained spellbound and

entranced, hearing nothing but the beating of our hearts.

We were at length called back to life by the passionate grief of old Armitage, who lay forward upon the table, his head on his arms, sobbing as if his heart were fit to break, while he gasped—"Oh! my boy! my boy! you will never come back to your old father—no! never, never more!"

Phil Blake and the boys tried to console him; but it was not until that young scapegrace Hal struck up his stupid nonsense of "Mind you don't wake the baby" that the old boy began to relax.

Then the Colonel gave us "The Gallant Hussar;" Phil and Jack gave their usual contributions; the Alderman tried "The jolly old sun," and broke down in the middle of it. Then he undertook to explain "why a lawyer was like a saddle of mutton;" though I confess the resemblance was about as clear to me after the explanation as it was before. Then we all sang "Rule, Britannia" and "God save the Queen," and so "shut up in measureless content."

Next day when we embarked the Alderman came aboard to say "good-bye."

The leave-taking between him and the two boys was most touching. As I approached I heard Hal say —

"If anything happens to me, dad, you'll *do* something for Jack, won't you?"

The old fellow growled in reply—"Don't talk d—d nonsense, nothing is going to happen to you. You'll come back a general, or a captain at least, and Jack will be a major-general. I won't forget him—make your mind easy about that." Then seeing me, he said, "Good-bye, Penarvon—you're the mother of the family—mind you look after these jackanapes, or never look me in the face again."

As we shook hands the last bell rang, and the Alderman went ashore. He remained on the pier to the last, a conspicuous figure amongst the crowd, waving his handkerchief to us. We gave him a parting cheer as the tug took us in tow; then the poor old man broke down and turned away. Hal broke down, too, and Phil and Herbert led him below.

I suppose you may get used to the climate of Egypt as it is said the eels get accustomed to skinning in time, but we had not time to get acclimatized, and the heat nearly settled us before we came to close quarters with the Arabs, who, to do them justice, fought like devils.

The story of the campaign has been told— better than I can ever hope to tell it.

We were foremost in the midnight march on Kasassin—foremost in the thick of the fray at Tel-el-Kebir, where poor Hal Armitage fell wounded from his horse in the first charge upon the Arab spears. In riding to his rescue

Herbert nearly came by his own death, and I was knocked over by a bullet in my ankle. We were all three left for dead upon the field; and, indeed, had it not been for Phil Blake, who, with the colonel's consent, organized a detachment at nightfall to seek us out, we must have died before the morrow. When they brought us within the lines Herbert was cold and senseless; it seemed as if every drop of blood had passed out of his body, but he was still alive, and that was all.

As for Hal, it was all over; he had been dead for hours.

His father's grief had been prophetic.

Vain now were all his riches.

All the wealth of the world could not buy back his son.

Alas! the poor old man!

CHAPTER III.

HERBERT'S ORDEAL.

" Anywhere—anywhere out of the world!"

HERBERT was sent to hospital at Cairo. The doctors said he had had a miraculous escape—that if the bullets had been fired with the express purpose of avoiding serious injury they could not have been aimed better.

Thanks to his superb constitution he soon rallied, and was sent home with a captain's commission to complete his cure.

Alas! he returned barely in time to follow his father to the grave, and to find his mother not only penniless, but overwhelmed with debt. Having nothing but his pay to depend on for a living for himself and a home for her, his resolve was soon taken. He sold his commission, purchased her a small annuity, and placed her with an old and faithful servant in a charming little cottage overlooking the sea, in her native village of Trepolyia, in the county of Cornwall.

He then came to London, where his first task was to seek Blake and myself.

Small wonder that he could learn nothing of either of us, since I was still lying in hospital, while Phil was invalided and had quitted the service.

Poor Jack's next task was to endeavour to obtain employment. Two or three hours every day were devoted to perusing advertisements, writing letters, and making personal applications.

He applied for the position of chief constable at Stow-in-the-Wold—of governor of the prison at Kirkwall. In vain!

He wrote stories of his military experiences, and sent them to the magazines. In vain! They were returned endorsed " Not suitable," or not returned at all.

He heard from his mother every week, but her communications brought only cold comfort. Her health was declining fast.

One Monday morning he missed the usual letter.

Next day there came a telegram from the village doctor—" Your mother is dangerously ill; come immediately."

He had scarcely read the message when he was on his way to the quiet village by the sea. Alas! he arrived too late.

For a time he remained at Trepolyia, dreaming the hours away, dawdling drearily by the coast, or aimlessly mooning over his mother's grave.

One day the good old doctor blurted out, "Mr. Herbert, you had better cut this at once. Go back to London; get to work—work of any kind—or you'll go melancholy mad."

Next day Jack returned to town and again resumed his weary fight with fortune.

From morning till night he was on foot seeking work of any description—here, there, and everywhere. All avenues seemed closed against him—all save one.

It did occur to him many times to write to Fairfax and ask him if he would take him in any department, but his pride intervened, and he could not bear the thought of meeting Clara Trevor as a dependant.

Too proud to importune former acquaintances, he was gradually drifting down—down in the whirlpool of the great city. At last he took to staying at home all day, and prowling abroad half the night, a prey to morbid fancies—fancies which sometimes lead to madness, despair, and death.

One night he had been moping alone for hours in the semi-darkness of his miserable garret, situate in one of the slums on the Surrey side of the river.

There he sat, looking at the Thames which floated on under the cold moonlight, as placidly as if the wind had never ruffled its surface—as if its ample bosom had "felt no age nor known no sorrow."

All at once he started up and ejaculated, "One moment, and it would be all over."

Putting on his hat, he descended the stairs and walked rapidly towards the bridge—"The Bridge of Sighs."

When he reached a central recess on the right-hand side he paused, and looking down, murmured, "Yes, there at least is peace."

At this moment the great bell of St. Paul's

struck the midnight hour, and he found himself mechanically counting the peals aloud.

Then a strange chord of memory was struck, and vibrated through him.

He remembered as though it were yesterday when he and his comrades marched over that very bridge on their way to Portsmouth, brave in all the panoply of war; horses prancing, banners streaming in the sunshine, the band playing "The Girl I left behind me." He remembered, too, the girl he had left behind him. She stood on yonder balcony, waving her handkerchief. Where was she now?

He remembered, too, the very night before they left England, how he and poor Harry Armitage, after the theatre, had gone to E——'s. He recalled the sweet music they had listened to. Poor Hal, he was lying low out yonder in the desert wastes of the Soudan, while he —

"An hour or two will make no difference, and I should like to hear ' That strain again, it had a dying fall,' he muttered, as he passed from the bridge, over the Strand, by the Lyceum, up Wellington Street, to the left through Russell Street, to the right, under the Piazza, and so on into E——'s.

How strange and changed it all seemed, or was it he who was changed?

The place was crowded with a frivolous mob of men about town. A horse-faced buffoon of the period arrayed in evening dress, was braying out a succession of brutal insults to distinguished statesmen.

By-and-bye, a brazen half-naked lion comique, supposed to be of the feminine gender, informed her hearers in a hoarse voice " That's how it's done."

After a time there was an exodus of the " swells," then a silence, then —

He was at the very back of the Hall, his arms were moodily folded on his breast, when the boys who sang so divinely two years before struck up the madrigal of " The Mother and her Child." It was the very piece of music he had heard when he and Harry Armitage had sat there together, the very one his mother used to sing to him when he was a child.

The melody was wafted to him uncontaminated by the smoke and the surroundings, fresh, and pure, and sweet as the summer air.

For a moment the "mother" rose to his eyes, and he was a child again.

Swallowing his tears, he muttered through his teeth, "Well, anyhow there's one comfort; I shall 'make a swan-like end, fading in music.' Let me get away, and have done with it at once." So saying he rose and moved rapidly towards the door.

Was it fate, accident, or the "divinity that shapes our ends, rough-hew them how we will," that at this moment projected him bodily against Frank Fairfax?

The manager exclaimed, "Herbert! I'm

glad to see you, my boy; not hearing of you we thought you were dead and buried months ago."

"No," rejoined Herbert, bitterly, "I live, sir, live, worse luck. But—there—there—I must be off. Good-night."

Fairfax looked at him from head to foot—saw his gaunt features, his great eyes starting out of his head, his long, unkempt hair, his seedy garments, and took stock of the situation in a moment.

With characteristic *bonhomie* he said, "Don't be in such a deuce of a hurry; remember we have not seen each other for two years or more, and have lots to talk about. Nay—nay—I don't mean to let you go so easily. I stay here; always do when I'm in town. I'm a late bird, and haven't supped yet, so you must come and join me." So saying, he took him by the arm, and led the way through a side door to the adjacent hotel.

In two minutes' time they were installed in the manager's private room, which was bright as a roaring fire and half-a-dozen wax candles could make it.

The table was laid for supper with all kinds of nice things.

"Here you are, my boy," said Fairfax; "Liberty Hall—every man his own butler." And he proceeded to open a bottle of sparkling wine.

"You are very good," said Herbert, "but, really, I can't stay; I have important business."

"Business be blanked," rejoined the other; "business to-morrow, pleasure to-night. I've got you, and here I mean to keep you. Here's to you," he continued, lifting a beaker of Heidseck.

Herbert lifted his glass in response, put it down untasted, and without uttering one word fell back fainting.

"Gracious God! what's the matter?" exclaimed Fairfax. "Wake up, wake up, boy." With that he untied Herbert's frayed neck-cloth, tore open his soiled and faded shirt (cruel tell-tale), rushed to the adjacent bedroom, brought out a flask of eau-de-Cologne, bathed the poor fellow's temples, sprinkled it over him, and supporting his head upon his chest, began to howl, "Oh! come, I say, Jack, never say die; it isn't fair to go dying this way. You shan't die, d—d if you shall!"

Gradually Herbert opened his eyes, looked round, and seeing Fairfax, says —

"I've been alone a good deal, and I'm not quite myself; and—no, no, it isn't that—I've been unused to kindness of late, and it is the kindness that kills me; and it—I—oh, Fairfax! Fairfax!" then he burst out crying like a girl.

The tears did him good, for he made a clean breast of it, and told Frank everything. He listened in silence, and then said —

"It's a lucky thing, my boy, that I met you; you are a deuced good actor, spoiled by being a soldier. Any blockhead can pull a trigger or cut a throat, but it takes brains to make an actor. Look here! I'm beating up for recruits; I'll give you three guineas a week to start with, and when you've rubbed the rust off I'll make an actor of you. Not another word; eat first and talk afterwards. For my part I'm hungry as a hunter, and could eat a horse behind the saddle. Try the fiz; it will set you going. That's right, there you are!" and he piled Herbert's plate and forced him to eat.

It was astonishing the change a hearty supper and a bottle of champagne made in him.

The two men smoked their cigars and had a night-cap each.

Then Fairfax burst out again —

"Make yourself at home here until we start

for the north. There! Silence gives consent; off you go to roost. You shall sleep in my crib to-night. Not a word—good-night, God bless you, my boy!" and so they parted.

Herbert, to thank God for the pleasant future that was dawning before him, not altogether without thought of Clara, and as to how that proud and imperious beauty (for so she appeared to him) would receive him in his altered circumstances. And so he mused and mused until he fell asleep, and dreamt that he was acting Romeo again to her Juliet, and crowning her with the golden laurel wreath.

CHAPTER IV.

MISS CHALLONER.

"Fate, show thy face; ourselves we do not owe.
What is decreed must be, and be this so!"

JACK slept far into the next day.

When he awoke his threadbare garments had disappeared, and a tolerably extensive wardrobe was spread out all over the room with a change of linen, &c.

He was a little "fogged" by the arrangement, and rang the bell. In a moment Fairfax himself appeared, bringing in a cup of tea, which he made Herbert drink.

"You've taken it out, my boy; it's nearly

half-past four," said he. "Now look here, old man," he continued, "we mustn't stand on ceremony; in the first place see if any of these traps of mine will go near you. We'll have an early dinner and go to the play. To-morrow we'll look up my tailors about your " togs;" your "props" I've seen about already. Meanwhile you must let me be your banker. There are £20; if you want any more, say so, and you shall repay me at your convenience. Now not another word. Dinner will be ready in half an hour," and before Jack could reply Fairfax left the room.

By that post he wrote to Clara, telling her of the advent of Herbert, merely stating that he had quitted the army and was about to take to the stage. He thought the news would please her, and it did. Dormant hope revived; at least she would see him once more, and then—ah, then!—well, we know that "Hope springs eternal in the human breast."

In a few days Fairfax's arrangements were completed, and he and Jack left town by the night express, getting to Rosemount at two in the morning.

Mrs. Macnamara's lodgings in St. Dunstan's Close had been secured for the new recruit, and Fairfax dropped him there on his way to the Theatre House.

When he got home Frank had a warmer greeting than he had had for many a day.

Clara was always glad to welcome him, but now she sprang upon him—she caressed and kissed him repeatedly. She hung about him, and cooed. She took off his coat and wrappers. She pulled off his boots, and patted his feet tenderly as she put on his slippers. She had prepared a delicious little supper with her own dainty hands. She fluttered about like a butterfly, but always ended by croodling up to him. He knew what it all meant, though they had not exchanged a single word about it. He merely touched most lightly on the subject nearest her heart, just casually remarking that Herbert proposed calling in the morning to pay his respects.

Once she was about to speak, but the words stuck in her throat. She merely kissed him again, and said, "How good you are!" and retired to rest.

Fairfax followed her example, and speedily adjourned to the Ghost Room.

Herbert again slept till late. Nature was recuperating herself for the weary nights when sleep never visited the anguished pillow. At last he was awakened by the cawing of the rooks from the adjacent Minster Gardens. The sun was shining through the old mullioned window, embowered in greenery, through which he caught a glimpse of the Cathedral. At first he had no idea where he was, but in an instant it all came back, and he sprang out of bed like a giant refreshed. He was strong and young again; when he looked in the glass he scarce knew himself. The squalid, hopeless, miserable past was left behind him like a hideous dream.

Then he thought of her, of Clara—how beautiful she was, how proud, how innocent.

He wondered if she ever thought of the poor soldier. They would act together, would be thrown daily in each other's society, and then—yes, then!

Anyhow it was his duty to call and leave his card; indeed, he had promised Fairfax that he would do so.

Notwithstanding his mind being thus exercised, his body asserted the right to be cared for, so he ate a hearty breakfast, dressed himself with unusual care, and when he turned out he was the handsomest young fellow to be seen that day in the city of Rosemount.

With a strange feeling of embarrassment

he knocked at the door of the theatre house, and enquired of Brown if Miss Trevor was at home.

Brown was heartily glad to see him, but replied that the young lady was out.

"She stayed till half-past one, sir," he said; "in fact, the chief kept the horses waiting half-an-hour, thinking you would call. Dinner's ordered for five, sir."

A little disappointed Herbert left his card and said —

"Will you say I called, Brown?"

Had Clara been at home—had they met alone that morning—but it was not to be!

He turned from the door, and once and for all the current of their lives was changed. He paused for a moment to look at the play-bill. All the old names were there, and one or two new ones which he did not know.

Then he resumed his walk.

Sauntering through the main street of the city he turned towards the right, passed over the river's bridge, and walked straight on till he reached the city's gates. Then he ascended by the Barbican, and strolled along the summit of the walls, which commanded a magnificent view of the adjacent country.

It had been his favourite walk when quartered at Rosemount. Here, many a time and oft, had he, poor Harry Armitage, and Phil Blake strolled in the gloaming to smoke their evening cigars. He paused to look into the Convent grounds which lay beneath. The nuns were moving noiselessly and listlessly to and fro, just as they were wont to move a year ago—just as their predecessors were wont to move a century ago.

The very last time he stood on this spot with his friends, night was falling, and the sisterhood were flitting about in the same ghostly, aimless manner as now, and he began instinctively to quote Maturin's fine lines —

" Yea! thus they live, if life it can be called,
　Where moving shadows mock the parts of men."

" Of women, you mean," interrupted Hal.

" Aye, very much women, dear boys," said Phil.

" Don't you know that it was here, in this very cage beneath our feet, that poor, fiery, frail Anne Bellamy fretted her heart out against the prison bars, till she burst forth and shattered her wings in that last fatal flight that ended in misery, and shame, and worse." And then he told them the story of the spoiled beauty.

Herbert remembered every word that Phil had said. He could hear the very sound of the rich musical voice.

Poor Phil! where was he? And what had become of *her?*

At this moment a young lady, clad in deep

mourning, approached. She was tall, and of distinguished demeanour. Lifting his hat he stepped aside to let her pass. As she did so she raised her eyes, the blood rushed from her heart to her face, as she exclaimed —

" Mr. Herbert ! "

" Miss Blake ! " he answered, in astonishment. " Good heavens ! How strange ! At this very moment I was thinking of you."

" Of me ! " she replied, in equal astonishment.

" Of you ; the very last time I was here your father stood beside me on this very spot."

" My father ! My poor father ! " she said, sadly."

Something in the tone of her voice struck him.

" Pardon me," said he, " you are in mourning. Is it for— ? "

" For both," she answered. " He came back from that dreadful Soudan death-stricken. Mamma tended him by day and night, and in less than a week after he had been taken from us she followed him; they share the same grave."

"Forgive me," said Herbert, "that I have recalled this great trouble."

"Trouble," she answered. "It is a relief, it is a pleasure to speak of him, and her, to one who knew them, and who loved him as I know he—he loved you. I am here amongst strangers, to whom I am unknown, even by name, and in all that pertains to my past life my lips are sealed."

"Amongst strangers!" and then he enquired with diffidence — "May I venture to enquire what has brought you here?"

"My profession."

"Your profession!"

"Yes. I am fulfilling an engagement at the theatre."

"At the theatre here?"

"Yes, here, sir, where once upon a time you enacted young Romeo."

"You astonish me."

"Oh! nothing more natural. I always loved the art, and when I found myself cast on the world I resolved to try the stage. One must live, you know. I had often heard papa speak of Mr. Fairfax, his kindness and liberality to young beginners, so after every stage-door in London had been closed in my face, I induced an eminent actress who had given me some lessons to accompany me to his rooms at his hotel in town, and he gave me an engagement there and then.

"I have been in his company more than ten months.

"If you are staying here to-night I hope you will come and see me act."

"I will not only come and see you act, but I hope I shall soon act with you."

"You—you!"

"Oh! yes. I sold out more than twelve months ago, and am going to tempt fortune on the stage myself—in fact, I am here now to join Mr. Fairfax's company."

"How strange," she said, as they walked back towards the city. "And what are you going to act, pray?"

"Whatever Mr. Fairfax chooses to give me. He says I am to begin at the beginning. And you—what do you act?"

"Oh, anything—everything, but I have already been entrusted with many very important parts."

"Pardon me, but I didn't perceive your name in the list of the company."

"No; my friend, Mrs. Vavasour, advised me not to act under my own name until I had made my mark, so even Mr. Fairfax himself is in total ignorance of my family or friends. I am known here only as Miss Challoner."

"Miss Challoner?"

"Yes, and you will oblige me by remembering Miss Blake only to forget her.

Please recollect that for the present I am simply Miss Challoner."

"I shall recollect," he replied.

Then they chatted about the theatre, about the company, about everybody but Miss Clara Trevor.

Strange, they both instinctively avoided all mention even of her name!

At length they reached the ferry-boat, in which they crossed the river; then, resuming their homeward way, they reached Precentor's Court, where Caroline lodged in an old-fashioned house, the first from the main street.

They lingered for a moment at the door, and, as he lifted his hat to turn away, she said —

"Now, Mr. Herbert, what is it Laertes says to Ophelia?—

"'Remember well
What I have said to you.'"

Placing his finger on his lip, he responded with mock gravity —

> " 'Tis in my memory locked,
> And you yourself shall keep the key."

Then, with a smile on his lips, he took one step into the street, where he encountered, face to face—Fairfax and Clara.

By some fatality they were walking their horses past at that very moment.

They heard the words and saw the action, though Caroline, who had entered the house, did not see them.

The interview, the incident, the words were all the most innocent things in the world, yet the whole affair was most *mal à propos.*

Herbert bowed to Clara and Fairfax, and made towards them to offer his hand, but they both vouchsafed only the curtest recognition and passed on.

Now five minutes' explanation would have made all right, but he had given his promise to Caroline, and felt himself bound by it.

As he strolled towards his lodgings he thought he would go back and ask her consent to his explaining the nature and extent of their acquaintance to Fairfax, and he returned to Precentor's Court for the purpose.

All at once it occurred to him that she might imagine there was something between him and Clara, which rendered such an explanation necessary; then he resolved that he would seek Fairfax at once and tell him that Miss Challoner was the daughter of their mutual friend, Phil Blake, and, firm in this resolution, he walked rapidly towards the Theatre House, reached the door, and—turned away.

"No, no," said he, "if I go volunteering explanations of this kind they will think there is an 'affair' between the girl and me. Let it slide."

Such accidents as these determine the

career of a life—a life did I say?—sometimes of many lives.

You go up one street or down another and you meet your fate in the shape of some fragile woman or some stalwart man. Had you gone down the one street or up the other you had perchance escaped a life of weal or woe.

I don't think Herbert knew his own mind when he sallied forth that morning. Had he called earlier at the Theatre House, had he not taken that walk upon the city walls, how different might have been the fate of all concerned.

He went home to his simple meal, but he did not enjoy it with the appetite of the morning.

When Clara and Fairfax sat down to dinner there was a death's head at the feast; yes, there it was, in the middle of the table, staring them both in the face. They couldn't eat that, nor could they eat much else at that sitting. Dinner was a failure.

When the cloth was removed, Clara said—

"Papa, will you do me a great favour?"

"Anything in the world, my darling, that I can do."

"Thanks. You told me this morning that Mr. Herbert was to open in Romeo next week. I don't care to act with amateurs; please don't let me play Juliet."

"My child," Fairfax replied, "do be reasonable; it will be one of the greatest houses of the season."

"So much the better; I shall not be missed, and you've promised, you know."

"Yes, I know I promised; but, good Heavens! what am I to do for a Juliet?"

"Oh! there's Miss Challoner, another amateur. They will understand each other admirably; in fact, they do already."

"Clara," said Fairfax, gravely, "don't talk nonsense. Herbert is a man of the world—has 'seen men and cities'—"

"And women too, I've no doubt," she answered, bitterly.

"Certainly, no doubt," replied Fairfax. "I presume he has met Miss Challoner somewhere in his travels. Surely there's nothing criminal, or even remarkable in that!"

"I did not say there was," replied Clara; "only it does not say much for his taste— an awkward, gawky, sallow creature like that!"

"*Chacun à son goût,*" muttered Fairfax, as if he were not altogether of that way of thinking.

"But, apart from that, I don't suppose Miss Challoner has ever played Juliet," he continued.

"Well, she has got a week to get 'up' in the part, and she can 'learn the drama's light from Romeo's eyes.'" And then Clara went to Fairfax and hugged him, and said, "Oh! papa, bear with me, for I am very unhappy;

never speak to me again about it. And oh! for Heaven's sake, don't ask me to play Juliet!" And then she rushed from the room.

Poor Clara! poor Fairfax! what more could he do to help her?

He lighted his cigar, unfolded his *Times,* and growled, "D—n the fellow! If I were his age, and only had the chance."

The following morning Herbert called at the Theatre House to pay his respects to Clara.

"Miss Trevor was out," Mrs. Brown said, curtly, "and Mr. Fairfax was engaged; but the stage-manager would acquaint Mr. Herbert with anything requisite to know about the business of the theatre."

Accordingly, to the stage-manager Herbert went. Mr. Tony Aston, a somewhat brusque and eccentric old man, informed him that he was to open in Romeo on the ensuing Monday, but that a rehearsal would be called to-morrow for him and Miss Challoner, who played Juliet."

The alteration in the cast astonished Herbert, but he had been a soldier, and he knew his first duty was obedience; so he heard all, and said nothing.

To his surprise, and, indeed, to the surprise of everybody else, Caroline was letter perfect in the text and thoroughly *au fait* in the "business."

It was the one particular part she had known backward from childhood—the one particular part it had been the ambition of her life to play.

Apart from all this, she had studied it with Mrs. Vavasour, besides which she had seen every actress of eminence who in her time had attempted Juliet.

As for Clara, if she were ungenerous enough

to have thrown up the part merely to spite Herbert (and she was only a woman!), she was "hoist with her own petard," for she had given Caroline a chance for which she might have waited for months—perhaps years.

Although Fairfax sympathized with his ward, he did not suffer his feelings to affect the interests of the theatre; hence he made a feature of Herbert's opening, assured that, for one night at least, his friends would crowd the house.

Then the local papers spoke of "Captain Herbert, the hero of Tel-el-Kebir, who had taken to the stage, and would appear in his magnificent impersonation of Romeo, so well remembered here," &c.

All the upper ten of Rosemount mustered in strong force. The Marquis of H—— and his family, the Lord Mayor and Lady Mayoress, the officers in garrison, and all the little big-wigs of the place.

The theatre was crowded, and Herbert had a tremendous reception. Poor Clara, sitting in her room in the Theatre House, heard it distinctly.

It was a night of triumph for Herbert, and a still greater one for Caroline, but of torture for Clara.

Perhaps, in her heart of hearts, she thought that Caroline would break down at the rehearsals, that he would come and beseech her to play Juliet. Perhaps she thought that the audience would resent another woman's playing her part.

Alas! the fickle multitude accepted the change with disgusting equanimity—even welcomed the stranger, and enjoyed the new sensation. It was hard to bear!

Fairfax saw it all—his practised eye detected genius in Caroline and power in Herbert.

He had much to learn, Caroline but little;

but when he had learnt he would tower over them all, that was Fairfax's opinion.

The furore increased act after act.

At last Clara could endure it no longer. Throwing a shawl over her head, she rushed from the side door of the house into the pit passage and leaped up the gallery steps. Olympus was crowded to the roof, but there she stood, at the back, amidst the great unwashed, and witnessed the last scene, until the curtain fell amidst a tempest of applause.

Then she sprang downstairs, returned to the house, bathed her face and eyes, and kept down her emotion as well as she could. For the future she resolved that her artistic ambition should triumph over her woman's weakness, that she would garner up her laurels; and that henceforth no one, man or woman, should rob her of a single leaf.

She bustled about and prepared Fairfax's supper, and when he came in, rather moody and depressed, she went up to him, bright and smiling, and putting her arms round his neck, she said —

"Papa, I've been very foolish, but oh! forgive me this once, and I'll never do so any more."

He kissed her, and said —

"Ah, my child, when you are older and wiser you'll know better. There, there, say no more about it."

On presenting himself at the theatre next morning, Herbert met with a cordial greeting from everyone but Clara, who sat alone at the prompt table.

When he approached to make his devoirs she rose and gave him the coldest, most chilling reception.

He tried to make conversation for a few minutes on subjects of general interest, but he might as well have tried to thaw the North Pole; so, finding every advance he made met with most freezing politeness, he took his departure, somewhat mortified. Pride, always his foible, but now his safeguard, came to the rescue, and he resolved henceforth to be as distant as she was; while as to Caroline— well, perhaps he had already compromised her by his indiscreet attentions. For the future it behoved him to be more prudent. Besides, had he not his art to occupy his thoughts and engross his mind? We shall see.

For the first week he had an easy time, too easy in fact. He went to the theatre nightly to see the performances, which he now regarded with especial interest, and justly so, inasmuch as nothing but the best pieces were selected, and they were performed in the best manner.

One morning Fairfax said to him —

" Now look here, Jack, I like you, and I like not everyone; and if you will be guided by me I'll put you on the right track, but we must have no illusions. Don't imagine that you can leap upon the stage, like Pallas from the front of Jove, and say, 'Hoop-la! here I am—an actor, ready-made!' Not so, my boy. Remember that 'Humility is the first step in the ladder of wisdom'; hence you must work morning, noon, and night if ever you mean to succeed. What is it Sir Joshua says—or is it old Bruin or Burke who says it for him?—'Excellence was never granted to man but as the reward of labour.'"

Herbert took this advice to heart, and profited by it. He was always ready to put his shoulder to the wheel in every department. If any member of the company was indisposed or unable from any cause to fulfil his duties, he was the stop-gap; if anyone was unable to study a long part at short notice, he came to the rescue.

With such industry, such ardour, and such modesty the result could not be doubtful.

And now help me, gentle reader, to leap over two years at a bound.

After a year of assiduous and indefatigable application Herbert had mastered the rudiments of his art. His muscles were entirely subservient to his mind, habit had become second nature—no occasion now to pause to think what to do with his hands or where to place his feet. He moved with grace, ease, elegance, distinction, and perfect harmony of motion. In a word, he had become an actor, and was now dividing public favour with Clara, with Caroline, and even with Fairfax himself.

Meanwhile the relations between those two young ladies had, unfortunately, not become more cordial.

Of course, Clara had a monopoly of nearly all the great parts, but Caroline's performance of Juliet (of which she retained undisturbed possession) brought her immediately to the front, and Clara found that by her own imprudence she had enabled her rival to leap at once into public favour.

Henceforth it was a fight between these two for fame, and something more precious even than that.

CHAPTER V.

MY OWN ORDEAL.

"Poverty abhor'd of men."

On my return to England I found that Jack had sold out, that Phil Blake was invalided, and that the regiment, or what was left of it, had been sent to the Cape.

I got Herbert's last letter from Cox's, and wrote to him there. I wrote also to Blake in Ireland.

Both letters came back, endorsed "Gone—address unknown."

I called on my old schoolmaster at Clapham—"dead!"

I went down to Sandhurst. Couldn't find a soul there who knew, or cared to know, me.

Hopelessly lame in my left ankle and suffering from a severe attack of bronchitis, I felt quite incapacitated for the active duties of my profession, and I, too, sold out.

As I was now living on my small capital it was essential to look at every shilling; hence I retired to humble diggings on the other side of the river.

Strangely enough, as I learnt afterwards, when we compared notes, I lived within a hundred yards of where Herbert hung out. Had I only known it what a blessing it would have been to both of us, but in London you may live next door—nay, in the very same house with your dearest friend, and not become aware of his existence. Anyhow, Jack and I were within a stone's throw of each other and didn't know it.

When his struggles were over mine were about to begin in serious earnest.

My father at one time had some little influence at the India House, and I thought his name might prove a passport to something in the Company's Civil Service. For upwards of two years I tried to obtain employment, but in vain. At length my little hoard was almost exhausted, and I had to look forward to a hopeless struggle for bread.

When I recall that time, without a friend—nay, even an acquaintance—no home but a miserable, squalid lodging, with a loud-mouthed, brutal shrew of a landlady, I wonder I ever lived through it. Fortunately I had my books, my blessed books—not many, it is true, but good—my pipe, my daily penny paper, and an occasional shilling or sixpennyworth in the gallery of a theatre.

Sundays I made a perpetual holiday, by every week seeking out a fresh place of worship, and thereby gaining many strange experiences which may some day see the light.

"When things get to the worst they must mend or end," and at length it pleased God to take compassion on my loneliness and my misery, and to send me succour in the shape of a—fiddler!

Amongst the extraordinary coincidences of Jack's life and mine the occurrence I am about to relate is not the least remarkable.

Jack's *Deus ex machina* turned up at Evans's; mine exactly opposite Sotheran's book-shop, at the corner of Lancaster Place.

One afternoon, loafing idly along the Strand, my eyes cast on the ground (for I was beginning to give life up as a bad job), I accidentally stumbled against a man, who exclaimed —

"*Donnerwetter!* can you not— *Ach! Mein Gott!*—it is Penarvon!" and I found myself being violently hugged and embraced by our late bandmaster.

A crowd gathered round us. They must have thought we were both mad, seeing two great bearded men hugging one another, and sobbing like a pair of hysterical school-girls.

Van Vort was the first to recover, and he said to the astonished gapers —

"Good people, it is mine comrade from the Soudan. We have fought together for your England. I thought him dead, and I find him alive. That is all!"

As he took me by the arm and led me down the Strand a cheer arose that might have been heard at Charing Cross.

The sound almost upset me, but Van Vort was steady as a rock, and I hung on to him and never let go until I came to anchor at his club, a famous theatrical rendezvous in the Savoy.

There he ordered dinner and wine, the best the place afforded.

Then he talked—ye gods! how he talked! He rattled off his own experiences without taking breath.

He had relinquished his appointment as

bandmaster of the —th, and was now leader of the orchestra at the Frivolity—a capital appointment. His manager was an excellent musician, and the most enterprising fellow in the world; his band was the best in London, and he was now engaged in composing and selecting the music for the new extravaganza, "The Banker of the Bosphorus." Then he enquired about my prospects.

By this time I had had a glass or two of wine, and I was really so glad to see the honest fellow that I told him exactly how I was situated.

"Ah," said he, "we will soon alter that. First we must send to Herbert."

"What about Herbert?" I enquired.

Then he told me all about Jack's career; he was the coming man, the biggest actor alive, and had great influence with his manager. Van Vort was sure he would find me a berth of some kind. There and then I wrote to Herbert, and next morning got a telegram from him in reply, urging me to come down to Rosemount immediately.

Without an hour's delay I left cruel London behind me, and when I arrived at my journey's end I found my dear old friend's heart and arms open to receive me as of old.

CHAPTER VI.

HER MAJESTY'S SERVANTS.

> " The actors are at hand, and by their show
> You shall know all that you are like to know."

JACK'S Benefit took place on the very night of my arrival. After introducing me to Mr. Fairfax (who received me with the utmost courtesy), he took me round to the front of the house before the doors were opened, and put me in the first row of the dress circle, where, luckily for me, there remained one seat still unlet. Presently in came the audience with a rush, and five minutes later the theatre was crowded in every part.

The play was Banim and Sheil's noble and almost forgotten play "Damon and Pythias." I forget what the after-piece was.

I had never seen the theatre, had never seen either of the plays, or any of the players before.

After the gloom and loneliness of my life in London the gay and exciting scene seemed enchantment, and when the curtain rose I was in Elysium.

Herbert acted Damon; a Mr. Bellhouse, Pythias; and Mr. Boanergus, before referred to, was Dionysius; Caroline was Damon's wife, Hermion; and Clara was Calanthe, the beloved of Pythias.

When the play commenced there was a short scene occupied by some of the minor characters. Then Herbert came on, and a shout of recognition arose which filled the theatre. At first he seemed as if his mind was so engrossed with the thoughts which were struggling for utterance that he was oblivious of all else, but the applause was so loud, and so prolonged, that he started from his reverie and bowed a brief acknowledgment.

Here I fear the captious critic and even the patient, long-suffering reader may be tempted to exclaim, " Confound the fellow ! what has this to do with the story ? "

Gracious critic, gentle reader, I wish to introduce my hero and my rival heroines just as they were introduced to me, and, furthermore, I want to endeavour to impress you as I was impressed on this eventful occasion.

If you object that " heroes are bores," I reply, " Speak for yourselves ! "

For my part I refuse to believe that an age which has produced and deified a Mazzini, a Garibaldi, a Lincoln, a Garfield, a Grant, a Gambetta, and a Gordon does not sympathize with heroes.

Without hero-worship there would be no

heroes. I am a worshipper. Jack is my hero and Clara and Caroline my heroines!

Of course you will retort with amused disdain, "My good man, gush as much as you please over a *soi-disant* soldier turned play-actor, and two young ladies, who, despite your rhapsodies, are mere country play-actresses, but don't expect us to follow suit."

Now here I have the advantage; you must either follow suit or throw up the cards.

> "You shall have the mustard,
> Else you get no beef from Grumio."

Abandoning metaphor, if you don't care to know what my hero and heroines are like, drop this book and take up another; if you do care, follow me while I endeavour to describe them.

To begin, then, with my hero.

Imagine, if you please, a man of nearly six feet, built in heroic mould, clad in the glorious garb of old Greece—an under-garment of some thin, delicate saffron-coloured material, relieved by a flowing robe of dark purple. A majestic head, with a profusion of brown waving hair, dashed here and there with gold. An oval face, with a delicate straight nose, from which radiated downwards from either nostril those two deep lines which emotion always appears to trace in the features of great actors; massive eyebrows, with long dark eyelashes, piercing splendid eyes; a mouth, firm almost to obstinacy, with the under lip slightly pouting above the dimpled chin; a fair, smoothly-shaven face, which scarcely revealed a trace of his rich brown beard, thus enabling him to the last to preserve the aspect of perpetual youth.

"Thro' his bright eyes Apollo beamed in light,
On his imperial brows Jove set the seal of might!"

Such was the picture of my dear old chum when I first beheld him on the stage, and for many a night after.

As the play progressed, Damon appeared to be in peril from some ruffian soldiers, and there came to his rescue a tall, handsome young fellow, hight Pythias, of fair complexion, well-featured, well-formed too, but, to my thinking, rather commonplace.

To him enters Calanthe.

The reader has met with Clara Trevor before, but no justice has yet been done to her marvellous beauty; bear with me, then, while I stay to describe her as she first burst on my enraptured sight.

Like Rosalind, she was "more than common tall;" and the noble undulations of her supple and ebullient figure revealed their statuesque outlines beneath her almost diaphanous robes of white samite and silver. Her face, which was of a pure oval, was surmounted with the brow of a goddess; her nose was short, straight, and delicate, with nostrils as mobile as they were transparent; while her dazzling teeth shone like ivory through the ripe, scarlet lips, which curved over them like the bow of Cupid.

"Then her neck, Jack, her neck!"

Her skin was white as alabaster, and surely she had the most perfect hands, arms, and shoulders in all the wide world!

Her eyes, luminous with liquid living light, were grey, or green, or blue, or brown, or violet, or all combined; her brows and eyelashes were black as the darkest night, and her beautiful head was crowned with a waving glory of red hair, bound with a fillet of white, and fastened in one huge knot behind.

Mark, gentle reader, her hair was none of your beastly Auricomus, but Red, real Red; the Red that Titian and Tintoretto loved to paint!

In the last scene, as she fell fainting in Pythias' arms, by accident or design the fillet burst, and when her glorious tresses streamed down almost to her knees, they literally covered her shoulders and his as with a flood of flaming sunbeams!

When she spoke, her voice, like Desdemona's, was "an alarum to love."

As for her smile, her lover spoke but prosaic truth when he exclaimed —

> " By the birth of Venus,
> When she rose from out the sea,
> And filled the Grecian Isles with everlasting verdure,
> Her smile, fresh from the soft creation of the wave,
> Was not more beautiful than thine,
> My own Calanthe!"

As she and her soldier-lover passed forth, the wife of Damon glided on, and twined her lovely arms round his neck, resting her superb head with its massive coils of blue-black hair on his broad shoulders. Dazzled and delighted as I had been with the glowing charms of Clara, I was profoundly impressed with the majesty and grace, the classic and imperial beauty of Caroline.

Two women so lovely, and yet of such opposing types of loveliness, I had never seen before, nor have I since. The one was "like the morning, dewy-eyed and fair; the other like the twilight, soft and dark." This striking contrast gave an added charm to both.

I suppose had I been cast the part of Paris, being myself as black as a crow, I should naturally have awarded the auriferous fruit to my golden-haired goddess.

When Damon and Hermion spoke they filled the air with music; and, as they moved, each step and every gesture recalled to my mind visions of "that marble majesty of the elder world," when Phidias devoted his genius to the "deification of man's strength and woman's loveliness."

I followed the progress of the play with continually increasing interest until it approached a termination.

Calanthe had been borne fainting from the stage.

"Beside the block the sullen headsman stood."

Pythias had nerved himself to die for his friend's sake. His comely head was bowed upon the block, the axe was uplifted in the air, the fatal blow was about to descend, when lo! the hum of distant voices—shouts, nearer, yet nearer still. Then an acclamation that shook the theatre, as the prison gates were dashed asunder, and in the centre of the stage stood a wild, demented man. His dress was torn to tatters, his head and neck besmeared by a bloody sweat, his hair dishevelled, his nostrils dilated, and his eyes ablaze. With a wild, maniacal laugh, which sent a thrill through me and through the house, his eyes flashed fire; his face became fixed; a convulsive quiver, a sort of *rigor mortis*, appeared to pass through every limb and every nerve; till, with a crash which seemed to shake the building to its base, Damon fell senseless on the stage.

The illusion was so complete, and the effect so awful, that I really thought that he was stricken dead, and was with difficulty restrained from going to his help.

Presently, however, he recovered from his swoon, and, recognizing Pythias, in a paroxysm of delirious joy he recounted how he had obtained the good steed, with whose timely help he had been enabled to return to Syracuse in time to redeem his promise and to save his friend.

At this moment Dionysius advanced and called upon the proud Pythagorean to redeem his word.

At the sound of the tyrant's voice, Damon sprang from the centre of the stage, and with one bound leaped upon the scaffold, exclaiming, "Lo! I am here!"

As the words left his lips he stood like a man transformed to stone.

The effect was electrical. The house "rose" at him, and the audience went mad with excitement; so did I.

In the end the friends were restored to life, love, and liberty, and amidst the general rejoicings the curtain fell.

I was so excited and delighted that I didn't care to see the after-piece; so I rose and left the theatre and strolled round the minster in the moonlight, smoking my pipe and thinking over what I had seen, till the streaming out of the crowd told me the performance was over.

I have dwelt at length upon the impressions of that memorable night, not only because it marked an epoch in this story, but because it was then that for the first time I saw the light of my life.

Ah! my darling! I loved you from that moment, and I shall love you until I die!

CHAPTER VII.

MY FIRST AND LAST APPEARANCE AS AN ACTOR.

"Fools rush in where angels fear to tread."

THANKS to Herbert's influence, my name was placed on the free list.

I was punctual in my attendance at the boxes every night. Sometimes I had them almost entirely to myself. On these occasions Jack used to call me the "box audience." More frequently, though, I was crowded out of sight, and was glad to squeeze in where I could.

There were three or four new pieces every

week. Think of that, *blasé* London playgoers, condemned to one piece for twelve months running!

Of course the accumulation of this abundant repertoire had been the result of years of labour; but the acting appeared so easy, so simple, so natural, that I needs must think it was the easiest thing in the world to do, and that I could go on the stage and act myself.

One day Jack came home sorely exercised in his mind at being cast " Joseph Surface," a part he had never acted, and one, moreover, which he detested.

Now, " The School for Scandal " was a play in which I took great interest, arising from the fact that in our regimental amateur performances, when I was in the Greys, I had acted " Careless," and, having a decent baritone voice, had not only sung the incidental song, " Here's to the maiden of bashful fifteen," but had actually got an encore for it.

Of course I duly recounted my "peaceful triumphs" to Jack, who used to banter me in his quiet, pleasant manner, and say, "I see what'll be the end of it, Bob—you'll be disgracing your family by going on the stage yourself."

"There is many a true word spoken in jest." I don't think I disgraced my family, but I certainly disgraced the stage by bringing upon it (I can afford to be candid now) the most arrant duffer that ever walked on two legs.

This was how it befel:—

On the morning of the production of "The School for Scandal" Bellhouse, who was the stock Careless, in going down the pit passage, sprained his ankle by slipping on a piece of orange peel, and had to be carried home. There was no possibility of his acting that night; hence it occurred to Jack that here was a desirable opening for me. So down he came to St. Dunstan's Close, dragged me up to the theatre, and, almost before I knew where I was, I found myself pitchforked on the stage rehearsing Careless. Of course I was letter-perfect in the words, and rattled them off glibly enough. I sang my song, too, without a false note. It was in vain that I urged that I was lame; Jack insisted that my infirmity was scarcely perceptible.

The whole thing was done so quickly I hadn't time to get nervous in the morning.

Alas! it was a very different thing at night. My delusion was roughly dispelled, and I was soon fated to learn the difference between an amateur and an actor!

A great house was anticipated; all the seats were taken for the boxes.

The play was a never-failing attraction when Fairfax played in it.

Charles was his crack part. Other Hamlets, Othellos, and Macbeths there were in abundance; but there was only one Charles Surface, and his name was Frank Fairfax. Besides this, the play was admirably acted and superbly mounted.

There was only one drawback—my unlucky self.

Jack was engrossed and preoccupied all the afternoon, having Joseph Surface on the brain. So was I; and by about five o'clock I began to quake.

I didn't know what stage-fright meant then. I know now.

Jack kept ominously silent, or spoke only in monosyllables. At last I could stand it no longer, so off I went, taking the precaution, however, to borrow from him a pair of shoes and buckles, a pair of white silk stockings, some ruffles, and other fal-lals.

I had looked out my costume in the morning, and left it in the spot assigned for my dressing-place.

When I arrived at the theatre the gas was

not lighted, so I turned out and took a stroll round the minster while I smoked a pipe. Usually the nicotian weed soothes me, now it only irritated me.

Back I went to the theatre. Found it still in total darkness; out again into the streets, until I fretted myself into a fever.

Another half-hour, then back again. At last the gas is lighted, only half-lighted though; 'tis a sort of darkness visible.

I grope my way down a long, gloomy, vaulted corridor to the dressing-room.

I am the first man in.

The place is awfully quiet, not a sound, not a breath is to be heard; there is something ghastly, sepulchral, and uncanny about the whole arrangement.

There are ten or a dozen wig-blocks, looking awfully like human spectral skulls, surmounted by white-powdered wigs; they are screwed on the edges of the long toilet tables on either side of the room.

Hanging up here and there are the embroidered coats and hats of a century ago; there is an eerie look about it all.

I find my way to my dressing-place (it is next to Jack's), and commence overhauling my costume; it is a queer, old-fashioned Court dress, a real one. I wonder what youthful macaroni was presented at Court in it, how many generations of Careless's have worn it before me, how many of them are living, how many dead, and where they are buried?

A lively train of thought I've got into certainly!

All at once it occurs to me that my unfortunate legs are not "things of beauty," and that I'd better cover them up before the other fellows arrive.

I begin to wrestle with Jack's stockings. There's room enough and to spare in the legs, but oh! my unfortunate feet!

At last I succeed in getting them on, and commence another tussle with my subligaculæ. I am rather ignorant of the geography of these unmentionable garments, but at last I struggle into them.

At this moment I look up towards the door, and as I'm a mortal man (don't laugh, reader!), I see, or think I see, the figure of a pale-faced woman in white in the doorway!

She is looking steadfastly at me. Evidently she is a well-bred woman, inasmuch as she has deferred her visit till I am fit to receive her as a gentleman should.

I advance, she retires. As I reach the doorway the lights go up with a sound like the whistle of a small steam engine. Then the sound of advancing feet, the hubbub of voices, pleasant laughter—the murmur of a gathering crowd in the pit passage underneath.

A minute afterwards and the dressing-room is filled with the " boys." I breathe again, although I am still puzzled to know what "The White Ladye" can possibly want with me.

I once thought of speaking to Jack on the subject, but concluded that he had enough on his mind already. As for the other fellows, I'd no desire to become the butt of the dressing-room.

Fact or fancy as the apparition might have been, it certainly doesn't help me over the ground either in my preparations or my subsequent performance. Jack could give me no help, and all the others were dressing away for dear life to begin the piece. They, however, left old Wigley, one of the dressers, entirely to me. Poor old Wig is normally imbecile, but on this occasion he is wholly idiotic, and "tight as a drum" in the bargain.

My next operation is to get on Jack's shoes, which are nearly two sizes too small, and give me "fits."

I have no wig, and it is necessary to powder my hair; of course I don't know how to set about it. Wigley suggests I should commence operations by anointing my head with bears' grease, but the powder won't adhere.

Accepting another suggestion from Boanergus, I plaster my hair with soap. The powder sticks fast enough then, I warrant you.

By this time the first act is over, the actors return from the stage, laughing and talking. I can't see what there is to laugh at; at any rate, I am in no mood for laughter.

The second act has commenced. "Now," I imagine, "I am sure to have the dressing-room to myself." A large, well-furnished room it was, but, confound the fellows! one half of them still remain to tell funny stories. I can't see the Joe Miller of their ancient "wheezes." "Why the deuce can't they go to the green-room?"

My hair, which curls naturally, is rather of a woolly texture—is utterly intractable, and sticks up and down in crinkly undulations; while, as to my face, in vain I plaster pigment over pigment, they only melt and burst out in blotches, leaving my black beard blacker than ever.

As I stand trembling before the glass, I contemplate the reflection with horror; there is no mistake about it, the "make-up" is a ghastly failure; I am more like a nigger than an English gentleman.

The second act is over now, and the call-boy sings out, "Beginners for the third act!"

"Good heavens!" I exclaim, "I'm on in the third scene! What shall I do?"

"Try back, sir," mumbles Wigley.

Happy thought! I will wash the beastly stuff off, and begin all over again.

Away I rush to the wash-stand, sluice my face with soap and water, rub it dry until it is red as beet-root, while "each particular hair stands on end like quills upon the fretful porcupine."

The actors—for they are all good fellows—cease to laugh at each other's jokes now; each one suggests his particular process of "making-up;" everyone begins to assist me, when lo! the call-boy makes the special call, always eagerly anticipated in this play —

"Mr. Fairfax's compliments, will the gentlemen do him the honour to take wine with him on the stage?"

At this summons I am left to my fate and to Wigley, who is now more idiotic than ever.

Two minutes later the call-boy returns, and roars out, "Mr. Penarvon! Stage waiting!"

Away I run as hard as I can split; in my haste I catch my foot upon a step in the passage; stumbling forward, I fall at full length, bursting Jack's unfortunate pumps in every direction, bursting every button about me, all over the place, bursting my knees out of my beastly breeches; the thrice-accursed things are tumbling down about me; I hold them up with one hand, with the other I try to pull up Jack's stockings, which are falling in festoons about my unfortunate spindle shanks, and with the cold sweat oozing from my face, which by this time is like a badly-boiled plum-pudding, my legs trembling beneath me like a pair of stuffed eel-skins, I stagger to my place.

I defy anyone to imagine a more woeful object than the unfortunate, half-dressed, wholly dazed, and utterly demoralized creature who now figures as the intimate friend of the elegant and accomplished Charles Surface.

When the scene draws off discovering the graceless scapegrace and his boon companions, there is an expression of delight, and indeed it is a pleasant picture which meets the eye, if I had only been in a mood to enjoy it.

Upwards of a dozen young fellows, attired

in the becoming costume of the period, overflowing with the exuberance of animal spirits, keep the table in a roar.

The central table groans beneath the weight of fruit and flowers and the choicest wines; the walls are covered with "the family of the Surfaces from the time of the Conquest" (for Fairfax is the author of the daring innovation of playing the drinking scene and picture scene together—an arrangement subsequently followed by various London and American managers, and described by those eminent authorities as being of their own original invention).

Amidst this flow of gaiety and brilliancy I feel like death at the feast, and my most fervent aspiration is that the stage will open beneath my feet and precipitate me into the depths below.

The wonderful ebullience of Fairfax, the peals of laughter which greet his every utterance, surprise and discomfit me.

In my fevered fancy I think that the laughter is directed at me. I stumble and stutter through my two or three first speeches, sticking at every word; then comes my song, and here even worse luck befalls me, for I start in a false key, come to grief in the very first verse, break down ignominiously, turn tail and bolt off the stage amidst a yell of derision.

I learn afterwards that Fairfax turns the situation adroitly by exclaiming, "Poor Careless! I fear he has taken one of these fellows" (pointing to a flunky) "for a bailiff. Never mind, I'll give you the song myself;" and he rattles it off with a life and go which carry everything before them. Young Howard, who plays Sir Benjamin Backbite, speaks the lines of Careless, and the play proceeds without my absence being further noticed.

Overwhelmed with shame and mortification, I rush to the dressing-room, tear off my traps, anxious only to escape before the actors leave the stage, determined never to show my face in the hateful place again.

As I am rushing out I encounter my angel, who is playing Lady Teazle. She's more beautiful than ever, but how stately she looks, how proud, how unsympathetic!

Notwithstanding my silent adoration for this glorious creature, I had never spoken to her in my life until that morning, when Fairfax introduced me. I could scarcely get a word out, still it was something to feel, to know that I was perhaps about to be brought daily in contact with her. I had given way to all sorts of foolish dreams and ambitious aspirations, and now it has come to this! Henceforth she will only regard me as the ridiculous amateur who had made an ass of himself. It is hard to bear!

As I pass by I lift my hat; I don't know whether she returns the salutation or not; I reach the door when a soft, sweet voice says, "Mr. Penarvon!"

I turn and look. Can this be the proud, unsympathetic Miss Trevor? She extends her hand; I come forward and bend over it; she continues —

"I am so sorry."

At the words I break down utterly, "Thank you! Good-bye! God bless you, Miss Trevor!" is all I can get out.

"Good-bye!" she echoed, in alarm. "What do you mean?"

"I mean," I replied, "that after this mortification and disgrace I dare not look any of these people in the face again. To-morrow, by the first train, I leave Rosemount for ever."

"You cannot be serious!" she exclaimed. "What has happened to you to-night happens to us all at some time or other."

At this moment Fairfax, accompanied by Charles Surface's servants, who carried the remains of the dessert, the flowers, and a bottle of champagne, approached the ladies' dressing-room and requested them to do him the honour of taking wine with him—a ceremony never omitted by the gallant Frank —and, indeed, one that formed part and parcel of the performance of "The School for Scandal" during all his *régime.*

"Oh! papa," says my lady Teazle, "Mr. Penarvon is so distressed about this unfortunate occurrence that he says he means to go away and leave us all at a moment's notice."

"Don't talk nonsense, my dear boy," rejoins Fairfax. "Don't talk nonsense. Any man who is worth his salt, anyone who has the highly-wrought nervous temperament which is absolutely essential to an actor, must be knocked over some time or other.

"Show me an actor who is not subject to stage-fright, and I'll show you an ass!

"Nay, more, show me a man who is incapable of stage-fright, and I'll show you an unsympathetic, unimaginative blockhead, who is incapable of ever becoming an actor!

"I made a much more miserable breakdown than you have done, the second night I ever tried to act. It was at Worcester—the High Sheriff's bespeak. I was playing a soldier (Howe's part in "The Sheriff of the County"), who has only a dozen lines or so to speak. I 'got myself up regardless' in a splendid military uniform—strapped up to within an inch of my life—ramrod up my back, busbie on my head, black leathern stock tightened round my neck, till I thought my head would burst and fly off.

"Down I walked to the footlights. As soon as I caught sight of the audience glaring at me deuce a word could I get out, good, bad, or indifferent. I merely stood still in the attitude of 'attention' and gasped, and I think I should have stood there gasping until now if the prompter hadn't called out very audibly, 'Now then, stupid! are you going to stay there all night?' Then I found my tongue, and replied, 'No! I'm coming off to punch your head,' and I did it, too!

"The operation was a sort of safety valve, but it was an expensive luxury, for it not only cost me my uniform, which burst to ribbons, but it also cost me my week's salary—(I was fined that amount!)—besides which I got notice to quit, and I should have been dismissed the company in disgrace if it had not been for the prompter, who, though a little crusty, was the best fellow in the world. He not only forgave me the licking, but he also interceded with old Bennett, the manager, to permit me to remain, and I stayed in the circuit for three years, till he and I (not the manager, but the prompter) became sworn friends and brothers.

"If you doubt me, ask Tony Aston, for he was the prompter."

At this moment the call-boy sings out, "Lady Teazle called for the act."

"Mind, you are to listen to papa, and to promise not to do anything rashly."

"Leave him to me, child, and go you away, or the stage will be waiting."

"Let the stage wait; I won't go till Mr. Penarvon promises."

"Ah, Miss Trevor!" I exclaim, "it is easy to promise to do anything you ask me."

"That is understood then," replies my angel, smiling on me like sunshine as she goes away.

Then Fairfax takes me to his dressing-room, soothes me with a glass or two of wine, draws me out and gets me to talk.

On one point I am quite decided; I will never put foot on the stage again as an actor —no—never!

It is in vain that he tries to talk me out of my determination; I tell him I would rather stand again unarmed and defenceless before a battalion of Arabs led by the Mahdi himself than I would encounter for a second time the awful ordeal of this more awful night.

Finding that I am fixed as fate on the subject, he replies —

"Perhaps after all you are right, my boy; anyhow, take my advice, give yourself a fortnight's holiday at Scarboro'; the sea breezes will blow the cobwebs out of your brains; by the time you come back here you'll be a new man and this affair will be forgotten."

Next morning I call at the Theatre House with Jack to make my adieux, and actually Fairfax and Miss Trevor accompany us to the station.

As the carriage rolls away she smiles upon me.

Who is cold and unsympathetic now?

"The White Ladye" had not brought me such bad luck after all!

CHAPTER VIII.

THE PRIVATE SECRETARY.

> "I once did hold it, as our statists do,
> A baseness to write fair, and labour'd much
> How to forget that learning; but, sir, now
> It did me yeoman's service."

SCARBORO' is the queen of the northern watering places, and a delightful spot I admit, but that fortnight was the longest I ever passed in my life.

At last one blessed red-letter day, to be remembered "to the crack of doom," I had a letter from Fairfax telling me that his private secretary had an offer to go to town, that the berth was open to me, if I thought it worthy of my acceptance.

Without an hour's delay I took the first train to Rosemount, and the very morning after my arrival was installed in my office.

Before he left for town old Gilbert, the departing secretary, initiated me as far as he could into my duties, and handed me over the keys of the check-boxes, the salary list, and the bank pass-book.

The position was one of great trust and confidence.

I had to take charge of the receipts overnight, to compare the tickets with the receipts, and pay them into the bank in the morning. I had also to write all business letters, superintend the giving out of playbills, see to the advertisements, and to hold the treasury every Saturday for the company and every Tuesday for the tradesmen.

Despite an occasional blunder or two, I had

the satisfaction of knowing that my services were appreciated by my employer, who at first seemed disposed to place "the pale spectrum of the salt" between us. His reserve, however, gave way to confidence as he perceived my industry and attention, and at length he came to regard me more as a friend than a servant.

Miss Trevor, too, who treated me at first with a little hauteur, when she found me patient, diligent, and unpresuming, began to thaw; then my natural taciturnity gave way, and I became more communicative, and endeavoured to make myself agreeable.

Although Fairfax had a wide circle of acquaintance, he had very few intimate friends. Three or four people were, however, free of the house, and they came whenever they liked and almost at all times.

There was Fred Bronson, the rector of the parish, who was a great authority on dogs and horses—never missed a meet, a St. Leger, or a Derby Day—was a capital man across country, and rode to hounds much better than he read the service. He had a splendid voice for a View hallo, but as for his sermons they were *vox et preterea nihil.*

There was his wife, a bustling little busybody, who, in consequence of having a craze for blue china and mediæval brasses, never could find time to keep Fred's buttons in order.

Then there was Canon Black, the Catholic priest, our next-door neighbour, as jolly an old boy as ever cracked a bottle or played dummy.

There was John Ralphstone, editor of the Conservative paper, who had been a barrister (it was rumoured that he had held a brief once), and who was the image of Tom Pinch.

Sometimes Mrs. Ralphstone came, although John preferred to leave her at Ralphstone Villa to look after the numerous and continually increasing olive branches, while he made a fourth at whist at the Theatre House.

I was occasionally invited to join these impromptu parties, and very pleasant affairs they were.

Having accommodating views on theological subjects, and going turn and turn about every other Sunday from one church to the other, I got on capitally with the priests of both denominations, being not infrequently invited to dine after the service with one or other.

When I dined with the Canon and his boys (*i.e.*, curates) I was always called upon (tell it not in Gath!) to take a hand at whist on Sunday afternoon.

Jack and I often used to turn in at the Bronsons', after the play, to smoke a pipe and drink a glass of beer, or gin and water, while Fred presided over the festive board (in the absence of Mrs. Fred), inhaling the nicotian weed from a huge churchwarden, and telling us racy stories about old times at Eton and Oxford.

Sometimes we used to change the venue by dropping in to supper at Ralphstone Villa—always sure of a hearty welcome, for Jack was a great favourite of Mrs. Ralphstone's, who scarcely ever missed a night at the play.

Our clerical friends were also very fond of the theatre, but dared not be seen there for fear of "Mrs. Grundy," although once, when Fairfax gave a ball and supper on the stage, they came and openly joined in the festivities, and flirted in the most audacious manner with our womankind, actually putting our noses out of joint altogether, always excepting Jack—dear old fellow! No one ever could put his nose out of joint with the girls.

While the Haymarket people were fulfilling

an engagement at Rosemount we went over to act in Barford for a few nights.

As there was no theatre there, we had to take over our scenery and fit it up in St. James's Hall, a large and magnificent building.

To our astonishment and delight, the Canon and his " boys," Bronson and his curate, turned up, in the most ostentatious manner, in the front seats on our opening night, and actually did not miss a single performance. To be sure, Barford was twelve miles from Rosemount, but it was not the distance that made the difference; it was because we were *not* acting in " that wicked theatre "—a nice distinction, truly !

During the run of a new play, written by one of our most distinguished authors (a play, I may remark, we produced for the first time at Rosemount), the hero was a young parson, an Oxford man, supposed to hail from Maudlin (Bronson's College), and he was naturally anxious to see how one of his own cloth would figure on the stage. Fairfax, therefore, arranged for Fred to enter by the stage door, so as to reach the private box without being seen by the multitude. There, ensconced behind the drapery and out of sight of the audience, he sat, enjoying himself like a truant schoolboy out for a holiday.

To our astonishment, however, he called to lunch at the Theatre House next day in a state of great perturbation, alleging that early that morning, just as he was about to sit down to breakfast, he had received a visit from three women—three loud-talking, impudent, but influential women, district visitors—who opened fire upon him, stating that they had been credibly informed by a pious apple-woman who kept a fruit-stall near the stage door, and who lived by disposing of her wares to the godless play-folk, that he had been seen on the previous night "entering the bottomless pit of abomination in company with that son of Belial, Fairfax."

Imagine the poor fellow submitting to this to avoid scandal!

He took it out, however, whenever he got a chance, for when away from home he never missed a single night at the play.

I had to call daily to leave my returns of the receipts. Sometimes Fairfax appeared out of sorts; then he would invite me to stay and smoke a cigar. On these occasions he would turn the conversation to my military experiences, which apparently interested both him and Clara.

I used to try to draw him out about his own reminiscences, which to me were a source of never-failing pleasure. At first he was somewhat reticent, but both Clara and I loved to listen, and when he was once set going he would talk by the hour and "act his young encounters o'er again."

What an ass I must have been not to have committed his strange adventures to paper just as he told them. Talk about romances! —why his life was romance upon romance; in fact, a perfect circulating library of them.

Then Clara! Ah! it was enough for me to be near her, to breathe the same air with her. But, oh! to sit at the same table, to hear her speak—these were foretastes of Elysium!

In her best mood she was bright as sunshine, and her conversation was as sprightly and entertaining as her manner was ingenuous and engaging.

Sometimes after dinner, during our discussions on the politics or literature of the day, she would take advantage of a lull, to run over to the piano, and play and sing like a nightingale.

She had one rare and remarkable gift—a passion for adapting poetry to music. If any particular poem took her fancy, she would commit it to memory, and recite it as the inspiration took her, improvising a running tremolo accompaniment on the piano. The effect was indescribably beautiful and touching; indeed, no other combination of melodious sounds that I have heard has ever affected me so profoundly. Sometimes she would finish with a march or a battle piece which would culminate in a Babel of warlike sounds; then she would leave the room with a joyous laugh.

Sometimes she would cease in a minor key, couched in a tone so low "that nothing lived 'twixt it and silence." Then she would remain for a few moments silent and motionless, and I could hear nothing but the beating of my own heart as she stole gently from the room.

That was the usual signal for my departure, when I too stole away, leaving Fairfax to his siesta.

In the midst of our most unrestrained

conversation I noted that if I merely named Herbert or Caroline a coldness would ensue, then a silence; so after a time I avoided all mention of them. At first I attributed Clara's strange demeanour to merely professional jealousy; but my eyes were soon opened.

Though Herbert had never spoken one word of love to either of these charming creatures, both loved him. Each divined the other's secret, and each was mortally jealous of the other.

He must have been blind as a mole, or else intensely preoccupied with his studies, not to have perceived the state of affairs. I think perhaps the latter, for at this period he was engaged morning, noon, and night in probing the heart of the mighty mysteries of Hamlet, Othello, Macbeth, and Lear.

Once, presuming on our long intimacy, I said to him —

"You seem fancy-free, Jack; do you never fall in love nowadays, old man?"

He replied with assumed gravity —

"Bob, a man whose heart is filled with a sublime ambition has no time to fall in love."

My heart was not filled with a sublime ambition, but, alas! it was consumed by a hopeless love which I could confide to no one. As for the object of my adoration, she did not even dream of the engrossing passion which had now become part of my existence.

Lookers-on see the best of the game, and I observed, that if Herbert said a kind word, or offered the simplest courtesy to one of these young ladies, the other fiercely, though silently, resented it.

Did he act a part with Caroline which infringed in the slightest degree on Clara's abundant repertoire, her anger was with difficulty restrained.

Did he act a part with Clara in which it was essential to appear ardent or amorous, it was a cruel wound to Caroline.

If he rehearsed a scene twice over with the one, it needed all the other's good breeding, to enable her to restrain her impatience within reasonable bounds.

Yet all these fluctuations of feeling, all these varying shades of emotion, were represented by nothing more than a look, a shrug of the shoulders, or a gesture of impatience. To me, indeed, they were as transparent as glass, as apparent as the sun at noontide; but then I loved *her;* nay, more, I loved them all, and my sympathetic regard for them enhanced the poignancy of my own sufferings.

The people by whom we were surrounded, however, except Fairfax (who, like myself, must have divined the truth), had not the faintest idea of the inception of the tragedy which was ripening to maturity before their eyes.

My lips were sealed, yet, in my own small way, I laboured incessantly to prevent misunderstanding, or scandal.

Herbert remained chivalrously courteous to both ladies.

Caroline was always equable, though sometimes coldly courteous; Clara, as the fit would take her, was like April: to-day, alternate cloud and sunshine; to-morrow, cold and cutting as the winds of March.

One day when she was April and March combined, I happened to be in the way; Herbert made a little "moue" at me, and whispered—"*Variam et mutabile semper Fœmina!* eh, Bob?" As a general rule, however, he bore these caprices of temper with imperturbable good humour.

So I watched and waited; hopeless for myself, yet not altogether without hope that I might be enabled to shield those I loved from consequences which I feared to contemplate.

CHAPTER IX.

AS YOU LIKE IT.

"But heavenly Rosalind!"

DURING the first year of my engagement the novelty of my position and the constant change of scene involved by our periodical visits to the various towns of the circuit, occupied my time, and occasionally diverted my mind from my own troubles. At length we returned to Rosemount for the ensuing season.

At this period Mr. James Clerehead, the erratic and enterprising manager of the Royal

Pandemonium Palace, the Megatherium, the Frivolity, &c., was beating up for recruits.

With characteristic modesty he had intimated to Fairfax that he was coming down to take stock of the company to see if there was anyone worthy of being picked up for his ensuing campaign in town.

In due course this gentleman turned up at the Theatre Royal, Rosemount, and it was my duty to escort him to a front seat which had been reserved for him in the centre boxes. A remarkable-looking person this! Slender, above the average height, a handsome head, sharp, aquiline nose, black hair, black moustache, dark eyebrows, piercing eyes, a pleasant cat-like smile, which seemed as if it might be perpetual, though I have seen it change into a tiger-like fierceness; a drawling but not disagreeable voice, and a habit of saying the most unpleasant things in the pleasantest manner possible.

The performance consisted of "As You Like it" and "Don Cæsar de Bazar."

The great *impresario* glanced at the programme, and muttered in the most *insouciant* manner, as if he were evoking an indolent blessing—" The Bard again ! —— the Bard ! These country actors have got their blessed Bard on the brain !"

Then turning to me he said, with languid insolence, " I say, sir, look here ; I've been travelling five mortal hours, and have only just arrived ; put me in a private box, and if I fall asleep come and shake me up when the farce begins."

Certainly this gentleman was not complimentary to our *corps dramatique*, but he was Fairfax's guest, and my orders were to offer him every attention. I took him, therefore, to the chief's own box, and left him there to sleep if he pleased, firmly resolved, however, that unless he snored loudly enough to interrupt the performance he might sleep till the next morning.

I had never seen "As You Like It," neither had Caroline. She sat next to me, and we both lost ourselves in the Forest of Arden and the fortunes of the hero and heroine, who played into each other's hands with a fervour and an artistic grace enchanting to behold— at least, to me—although I fear Caroline did not contemplate the process with so much equanimity.

I suppose I ought to have been jealous, but I knew Jack didn't love Clara, while Caroline was not altogether so sure of that.

Rosalind's love at first sight for Orlando, their after meeting in the forest, the ebullience of innocent wantonness and animal spirits in which she absolutely revelled during the mock love-making, the ecstasy of passion which lighted her eyes, illumined her features, and appeared to thrill through her very veins at the coming and going of her young paladin, the fainting when Oliver recounts his brother's peril, and the delightful manner in which she spoke the epilogue, are all as fresh in my mind now as when I first saw and heard them.

I shall never forget her entrance as Ganymede.

She was indeed "Jove's own page."

Her gorgeous and glowing beauty, her superb and symmetrically formed limbs, her exquisitely undulating movements, the indolent grace with which she lounged about the forest, all combined to form a most perfect incarnation of statuesque grace and feminine loveliness.

I believe Herbert made an admirable Orlando, but I confess I had eyes for no one but "the fair, the chaste, the inexpressive she."

Whether Clerehead slept during the early

portions of the play I know not, but I do know he was wide awake enough when Clara came on in the boy's dress.

He sat eagerly forward, craning his long neck out of the box, and never took his eyes off her.

While she was speaking the epilogue I remained entranced, and Caroline sat quivering and moaning like a wounded doe.

As for him, the fellow looked for all the world as if he would have leaped upon the stage, and in the " sight of all Israel " have claimed the guerdon Rosalind proffered to " so many as had beards that pleased her," though apparently he thought better of it, for that time at any rate.

When the curtain fell Caroline gave a little shudder, and unconsciously murmured to herself, though loud enough for me to hear—

"He must love her! Who could help loving her, so happy, so beautiful? While I—"

Then the band struck up, and I heard no more.

"As when a well-graced actor leaves the stage," so did "Don Cæsar de Bazan" appear to me a tedious, irrelevant, and impertinent burlesque; but I was in the minority, for the audience accepted the play, and Bellhouse, who played the hero not only with fervour, but enthusiasm.

Evidently Clerehead was favourably impressed also, for he engaged Bellhouse there and then at a very handsome salary, and a fortnight afterwards he left us to become *jeune premier* at the Frivolity.

That night Herbert and I were invited to meet the Metropolitan manager at supper at the Theatre House.

The invitation was made at his special request, in order that he might be introduced to Jack. The truth was, the astute *impresario* had been, to use his own elegant phraseology, "struck all of a heap" by both Clara and Herbert, and wanted to secure them both for the Frivolity.

Clara was at her best and brightest.

The great triumph she had achieved as Rosalind, Herbert's association with it, the sympathetic ardour with which he had acted up to her, the perfect semblance of reality with which he had invested the amorous utterances of the love-sick Orlando, combined with a certain speechless but persuasive gallantry which exhaled from him unconsciously, and which was part of the man's "loving, noble nature," set her thinking. "Could she have been mistaken about Caroline? Could he, after all—?" Then she thought —

"Sufficient for the day is the evil (or happiness) thereof. Let me eat, drink, and be merry; to-morrow I may die!"

So she laid herself out to conquer, and when she was in that mood no woman could be so agreeable, so seductive, so dangerous, or so irresistible.

I had never seen her so charming before. Clerehead told me long after that he had never seen anyone so charming in his life.

Fairfax was delighted to see her so like her old self. I, alone, was the death's head at the feast.

It seemed very hard to know that the other girl was breaking her heart for Jack, that he loved neither of them, and that my latest glimpse of hope was fleeting away from before my eyes.

If he loved her, and if she could be happy, I could have borne it with patience, if not with equanimity; for, after all, what was I to stand between them and happiness?

In business Clerehead was a man of few words, and after supper he came straight to the point.

Without ceremony he offered Clara and Herbert their own terms, to commence as soon as Fairfax could spare them.

Now the truth was that the Frivolity had an evil odour in the "chief's" nostrils, and on no account would he permit his darling to be mixed up either with the theatre or the associations which surrounded it. So he gave a point blank negative; and Herbert, thanking Clerehead very much, followed suit.

Then we bade "Good-night" to all, and wended our way homeward.

CHAPTER X.

THE LEGACY.

Next morning Fairfax turned out in pink with Clara; and a little baronet (jocularly known as the "Gipsey"), who had been a comrade of ours in the Soudan, gave Jack a mount, so he rode to hounds with them, and a very distinguished trio they made.

I fear that Caroline was more impressed than gratified by the little cavalcade as she saw them ride by Precentor's Court, laughing and talking, evidently in the highest spirits; while for my own part I must confess their laughter found no echo in my heart.

After I had counted my checks and written my letters I read the following remarkable advertisement in the *Times*:—

"If John Herbert, Esq., late Captain in the —th Lancers, will immediately communicate with Messrs. Wharton and Blogson, solicitors, 29½, Lincoln's Inn Fields, he will hear of something greatly to his advantage."

Without waiting for Herbert's return I telegraphed in his name, to this effect:

"Shall be glad to hear from you *in re* advertisement in to-day's *Times*."

An hour later I received a reply worded thus :—

"A legacy of £10,000 awaits you here. Kindly come to town immediately, or place us in communication with your solicitors."

When Herbert returned from the hunting field I showed him the advertisement and the telegram.

He was for rushing off to Fairfax at once to obtain permission to get away that very night, but I dissuaded him, alleging that it might be a hoax, or some artifice of Clerehead's (who had the reputation of being a practical joker) to get him up to town in the hope of inducing him to accept the proposed engagement at the Frivolity. Besides, it was impossible for him to be out of the bill for the ensuing week. The programme was published, and I knew that no amount of persuasion could induce Fairfax to alter it. I wrote, therefore, by that night's post to my father's solicitor, desiring him to communicate with Messrs. Wharton and Blogson, and to acquaint us with the result by wire.

Next day Mr. Stanton telegraphed me:—

" Have seen Wharton and Blogson. Legacy quite *bonâ fide.* Your friend had better come up to town as soon as possible."

Herbert obtained a week's leave of absence

upon important family business, and on Sunday afternoon he went to London.

Tuesday morning brought me the following letter:

"Tavistock Hotel,
"Monday.

"My Dear Bob,

"It's all true—there's no mistake about it. Your friend Stanton took me this morning to Wharton and Blogson's, where I saw a mummified old duffer who told me that ten thousand pounds had actually been bequeathed to me by a client of his, and who do you think it turns out to be? Why, Harry Armitage's father! The poor old boy died three months ago.

"Beyond this, I could obtain no information from the ancient idiot.

"Stanton seemed to understand him, however, so I've left the matter in their hands.

"The money is to be transferred to my

account at Swan's bank, with as little delay as possible, and to-morrow I am to sign certain documents. Meanwhile, Stanton has opened an account for me at Glyn's, and I've a cheque-book, if you please. Only think— a cheque-book once more!

"I'm now off to dine with Clerehead, and to-night we are going to see the slender Sarah, with the voice of gold, in 'Hernani,' and Clerehead has promised to introduce me after the play. Better keep all this to yourself till I come back. Meanwhile, 'to the last syllable of recorded time,'

"Believe me, always your own old

"JACK."

CHAPTER XI.

THE PASSING OF FAIRFAX.

> "But now, farewell! I am going a long way,
> Where falls not hail, or rain, or any snow,
> Nor ever wind blows loudly."

I got Jack's letter, as I have said, on Tuesday, and on Wednesday—alas!

Let me think where and how to begin.

It was the first meet of the season with the Marquis of H——'s hounds.

Now, Fairfax's mare, having cast a shoe the previous night, was not "fit," so he asked "The Gipsey" to give him a mount.

Unfortunately, our little friend had in his stud a vicious beast, called " The Roarer." The baronet rather liked to take it out of this brute, and whenever he got his knees into her ribs, she knew she had found her master.

I believe had Sir George got astride, the eternal devil, his Satanic Majesty, with all his host to aid him, couldn't have shaken him off. But then " The Gipsey " barely turned nine stone, and was under thirty years of age, besides which he was the best horseman in the county. Now, Fairfax turned twelve stone ten, and was over fifty.

As ill-luck would have it, this infernal brute, full of corn and devilry, was selected by Sir George's loafing scoundrel of a groom for Fairfax's mount.

I was in attendance to take my instructions, as usual, for the day.

Generally " the chief " was bright and

jovial; on this occasion I found him preoccupied and depressed. After we had finished our business, I ventured to observe —

"You seem rather unwell to-day, sir."

"Oh! I'm well enough in health, but I'm a little depressed in spirits, and I —" He started up and walked across the room once or twice; then facing me he inquired abruptly —

"Do you believe in ghosts, Bob?"

"I hope in them," I replied; "but I'm not quite sure of my belief in anything; I wish I were!

"Once, ever so long ago, I thought I saw my mother, but my father persuaded me that it was an hallucination. My poor mother had promised if she ever could come back, that she would be sure to come to him, and as he had never seen her, he was convinced I had been dreaming. But why do you ask me, sir?"

"Because—because I believe in indigestion

and nightmare—but I don't believe in ghosts, and yet —

"Of course, you've heard all the rubbish about the Ghost Room and the White Ladye?"

" I have."

" The very first night I slept there, a dear, dead friend appeared to me. I certainly thought I was awake, but what is it Hobbes says? 'To say one hath seen a vision or heard a voice is to say he hath dreamed between sleeping and waking.' So I suppose I was dreaming.

" That was five years ago.

" This morning I dreamt that *she* came again to the foot of my bed. Looking upon me very sadly, she murmured in the soft, sweet voice I remember so well —

"' Don't go out to-day, Frank—don't go out.'

" I heard her as clearly as I hear myself now. In the effort to reply, I awoke, and sprang out of bed. It was broad daylight, but I tell you, Penarvon, for one moment I saw her as clearly as I see you now. Yes, there she stood, with her fair hair and her dark eyes, her white dress and black ribbons. As I approached, she changed, as if by magic into the figure of a nun, with a child in her arms. For a moment, I stood awe-stricken, then I advanced, and *she, it*—what shall I call it?—faded into air! Now, what do you think of that, Bob?"

"I think you are a little out of sorts. We were up rather late last night. Perhaps a touch of dyspepsia. If I were you I'd stay at home this morning. Let me send the horse back to Sir George. I'm sure you are not fit to go out."

"Not a whit," he replied, quoting Hamlet gaily and glibly. "'We defy augury—there's a special providence in the fall of a sparrow. If it be now, 'tis not to come; if it be not to come, it will be now; if it be not now, yet it will come; the readiness is all.'" And so, with his usual buoyancy, he went forth.

Before he mounted, Clara said, "Papa, I don't like the looks of that mare."

"Nor I either," said I. "Just look at her ears; do let me send her back."

Whether through thoughtlessness, indolence, or mischief, the groom replied, "She's as right as a trivet, sir; Sir George rode her to hounds three days ago, and she went like a lamb."

Fairfax looked as if he himself didn't much like the appearance of the beast, but I suppose, after our conversation, he didn't care to show the white feather; anyhow he mounted, and away they went, apparently elate and confident, and a charming picture they made as they rode down the High Street.

I can see them now. She in her flowing habit, and he in his white hat, pink coat, a flower in his button-hole, well-cut boots and continuations.

I am not superstitious, but a presentiment of some impending calamity overshadowed me as they passed out of sight.

An hour later, as I returned from the Bank, I saw a group of stragglers coming towards the Theatre House, looking backwards at a waggon which was followed by an enormous crowd.

When the cart halted at the door, I looked beneath the tilt, and there I saw poor Fairfax extended at full length, his hunting dress all bestained and bedraggled with mire, his face wan and motionless, his eyes closed, his head resting on Her lap.

She sat behind him, her eyes fixed, her features ghastly pale, her beautiful hair all dishevelled and streaming over her.

The company being engaged with the rehearsal, were fortunately all on the spot. They came crowding down to assist in carrying the "chief" into the house.

Forgetful of everything but Clara's trouble, Caroline sprang forward to assist her, but she shrank from her, and clung almost by instinct to me.

The "boys" carried our poor friend to the Ghost Room, where we undressed him and got him into bed before the doctor arrived.

During this time Clara had suffered Mrs. Brown to conduct her to her own room, where, taking off her riding habit, she slipped over her a loose dressing-gown. Then she came rapidly down, and dashing open the door, stood among us.

"Well?" she said to the doctor.

"Patience! my dear young lady, patience!"

"Preach patience to the winds," she exclaimed; "but tell *me* the truth—is it life or death?"

The doctor replied, "While there is life there is hope."

"Yes," she replied, bitterly, "much hope! I see it in your eyes. How long will he last?

Is it to be to-day, or to-morrow, or next week? For God's sake, say when!"

The doctor hesitated before he answered.

"Since you insist upon knowing the truth, Miss Trevor, it may be a day, a week, or an hour. Meanwhile let us be thankful that he suffers no pain."

"Thank God for that! There is nothing more to be done, then?"

"Nothing."

"Thank you," she replied; "and now leave me, if you please, all except Mr. Penarvon."

I whispered the doctor to telegraph Herbert to come immediately, and then I sat with her through the long dreary night.

By degrees I learnt the truth from her disjointed exclamations.

They had not got clear of the city, and were descending a street paved with large granite stones—stones that were slippery and greasy.

Just at the very moment when both horses were struggling to keep their feet, Fairfax drew his white kerchief from his breast pocket, and as he flapped it out, a large plate-glass window opposite unfortunately reflected it. "The Roarer" caught sight of the reflection, shied, took the bit in her mouth, bolted to the right and over the bridge, as if a pack of wolves were at her heels.

Off she went, at a wild, mad gallop, and was out of sight in less than no time.

When she overtook them, half an hour later, she found him lying across the highway, speechless, senseless, his face quite rigid, his teeth clenched, the reins still in his hand, and "The Roarer" quietly browsing by his side.

After she had told me this, except for the tolling of the minster bell, which marked the progress of the hours, the silence was broken by nothing but the quiet breathing of the dying man. She had ceased to sob or moan, and merely sat beside him, her eyes fixed on his impassive face, pressing his hand in hers, and nursing it on her bosom.

Hour succeeded hour, until at length the great bell of the minster struck four — presently the chimes told us it was half-past the hour. The train from London was overdue!

Up to this moment Fairfax had not uttered a single word, but now, through the silence, his voice rose loud and clear —

"He's coming!" he cried. "Hush! hush! I hear his footsteps!"

I had not heard a sound to break the stillness of the dawning day, nor had she; but even as the words were uttered, Herbert, pale and breathless, stood upon the threshold.

The eyes which had been closed for hours now opened wide. As Herbert threw his arms around him he said, "Jack! dear old

Jack! I always loved you from the first, and I couldn't die till I had seen you."

Turning to Clara, he continued, "My darling, kiss me! Yet again! When I meet your mother in Heaven I can tell her I have done my duty to her child."

Then he fell back upon his pillow, and was silent for a time.

Presently they heard him murmuring to himself,-in a dreamy far-off way, "It was ever so long ago—we were boy and girl together—her hair was fair as morning, her eyes were dark as night—a white frock and black ribbons—"

He closed his eyes, and his breath came and went so regularly that it seemed to us as though he were sleeping.

Another hour! Another still!

The minster bell struck six; the sound appeared to have awakened him. Looking eagerly forward, and gazing into space, as if apostrophizing someone or something we could not see, he murmured—"I'm coming, darling, I'm coming."

And so he passed away, the old sweet smile upon his lips, while the bright eyes looked forth into the daylight where darkness never comes.

CHAPTER XII.

AT REST.

"Earth to earth may return, the material to matter ;
But high from the grave soars the spirit above :
His ashes the winds of the tempest may scatter,
The Life of Eternity lives in his Love."

SCHILLER.

ON the morning of the funeral, when Herbert, the Canon, and I went to take leave of our poor friend, we found Clara seated by the coffin, her eyes fixed on him.

Not a wrinkle or a trace of care was left upon that marble brow. A smile was on his lips—how young and beautiful he looked.

When we sought to lead her forth, she rose

and kissed the dear dead face, as she made moan —

"Oh! my dearest dear. My father and my friend, must I lose you? But it cannot be for ever!"

"It is not for ever, child, be sure of that," replied the Canon. "'He is not dead, but sleepeth.' Come then, come!" And so we led her forth—looking upon him to the last.

It was a day of dole in the city; the very elements seemed to have gone into mourning. The heavens were "hung with black," and the rain fell in one incessant, drizzling downpour.

All the public offices were closed, the flag on the Castle hung half-mast high, the great bell of the minster tolled during the progress of the funeral *cortége*. The bells of all the city churches were muffled, and rang out in doleful answer. It was, indeed, a day of lamentation.

The chief mourners were Herbert, the Canon, Ralphstone, Sir George, Clough, the banker, Walton, Fairfax's solicitor, and myself.

The men of the company, bearing a profusion of wreaths and bouquets, prepared by the loving hands of the women, came next. Then came the Mayor and Corporation, the Marquis of H——, the clergy of various denominations, besides which several of the county families sent their carriages.

Many of the officers in garrison followed.

Despite the rain, a vast concourse swelled the sad procession, which, by the time it reached the cemetery, numbered many thousands.

Our poor friend was beloved of the people, and it was quite touching to note the general grief of old and young—especially the women. Generations of both men and women had risen up around him from childhood, and they had grown to love him with their growth.

He had been conspicuous amongst them so long, "wearing the grand old name of gentleman" without reproach or stain. He was so kind, so charitable, so good to the poor; so generous, so lovable as a man; so accomplished as an actor; then the glamour of the stage had invested him with such a halo of romance, that it was no wonder that to their simple minds, he appeared the incarnation of all that was noble, and gentle, and gallant, and tender, and true! They loved him as one who belonged to themselves, as one near and inexpressibly dear, and his loss was so sudden and unexpected—his death so terrible—that it enhanced the poignancy of the general grief.

When we left the church the darkness was almost that of night.

Notwithstanding that the rain fell heavier than before every head was bared. Not a sound could be heard except the continual downpour.

At length we reached the grave.

Bronson commenced the remainder of the ritual—I have said before he had a marvellous voice—but, poor fellow! he was unequal to the task. As he uttered the words, "Earth to earth, ashes to ashes, dust to dust," at the sound of the dull thud of the earth falling upon the coffin, he faltered, turned pale as death, and broke down utterly.

Even at that very moment the rain ceased, the rift was lifted, the clouds vanished as if by magic, the sun burst forth bright and glorious, and he resumed his task, intoning trumpet-tongued the inspired promise of immortality.

As he ceased, the multitude bowed their heads in solemn silence; when, lo! the Bow of the Covenant arose and encircled the horizon with its many-coloured glories as if it were a sign sent from Heaven in answer to our prayers.

I cast upon the coffin a huge cluster of forget-me-nots and violets from Clara; Herbert followed with a wreath of laurel sent by Caroline; then the hush broke, the weeping crowd pressed round, and covered the open grave with flowers; and, with their sobs and lamentations ringing in our ears, we left our dear master to his last sleep.

END OF VOL. I.

www.ingramcontent.com/pod-product-compliance
Lightning Source LLC
Chambersburg PA
CBHW021827230426
43669CB00008B/886